BATHROOM BOOK
of
CANADIAN TRIVIA

Angela Murphy

BLUE
BIKE
BOOKS

© 2005 by Blue Bike Books
First printed in 2005 10 9 8 7 6 5 4 3 2
Printed in Canada

The Publisher: Blue Bike Books

Library and Archives Canada Cataloguing in Publication

Murphy, Angela, 1946–
    Bathroom book of Canadian trivia / Angela Murphy.

(Bathroom books of Canada ; 1)
ISBN-13: 978-09739116-0-2
ISBN-10: 0-9739116-0-3

    1. Canada—Miscellanea. I. Title. II. Series.

FC60.M87 2005   971   C2005-905599-5

Project Director: Nicholle Carrière
Project Editor: Audrey McClellan
Illustrations: Roger Garcia
Cover Image: Roger Garcia

Dedication

This book is dedicated to my fellow "Red Hats": Darlene, Deborah, Glenda, Janice, Lou-Anne, Moira and Roberta —ever thoughtful, always fascinating and never ever trivial.

CONTENTS

WE LOVE OUR FOOD!

BACK IN THE DAYS...

BOOZE & SMOKES

WILDLIFE

ODDS 'N ENDS

Acknowledgements

To the following people who contributed data, wisdom, clarification, comments, suggestions or entries for this book:

- To Peter, as always, for unfailing support in the face of yet another can of soup for dinner.
- To Audrey McClellan who managed to make a real book out of my ramblings.
- To the following people who contributed data, wisdom, clarification, comments, suggestions or entries for this book:
- Karen Blatz, Blatz Bison Ranch, Fort St. John, BC
- Delon Chan, Agriculture and Agri-Food Canada
- Detective Todd Cowley, Winnipeg Police Auto Theft Division, Winnipeg, MB
- Alan Jones, coordinator of Public Avalanche Warning Services, Canadian Avalanche Centre, Revelstoke, BC
- Margaret Kelly-Smith, Nepean, ON
- Bernadette Larivière, Gatineau, QC
- Ryan LeBlanc, Thunder Bay, ON
- Sarah Mosley, Winnipeg, MB
- Tim and Leslie Pogue, Calgary, AB
- Jim and Johanna Rodger, Argyle, MB

INTRODUCTION

An entire book dedicated to trivia is somewhat like a party in honour of solitude; a picnic celebrating rain; a school awarding stupidity; a steam bath in the tropics; a screen door on a submarine. In other words, useless, disadvantageous, impractical, purposeless, counterproductive, nonfunctional, meaningless, futile, expendable, valueless....

Sorry, but this is what happens when you spend month after month compiling, sorting, weighing and précising thousands upon tens of thousands of facts—or, in newspeak, "factlets," which are apparently even smaller.

I've become a pariah at parties, where other guests avoid eye contact with me, fearing it will somehow be taken as an invitation for me to tell them the percentage of people in Canada who drink the gimlet they're holding as opposed to the martini in my hand or how many droplets of water it takes to make one ice cube or that there is a one in five probability that they didn't shower before leaving the house.

Friends have stopped calling, or if they dare to get in touch, they suddenly remember they're late for an appointment if I even breathe the phrase "Did you know...?"

My family, poor innocents, don't know that, despite how thrilling it would be, they are not likely to see a cougar in their backyard. They also haven't the faintest idea that they have only a one in 30 million chance of becoming prime minister, and if one of them were elected to lead the country, they would be obliged to live at 24 Sussex Drive, a house that is reportedly haunted by the ghost of Anne, wife of John Currier, a former member of Parliament who built the house for himself in 1866.

My husband tells me I have so many facts in my head I'd be a shoe-in on Jeopardy. The origin of that phrase, by the way, tells us that we've been spelling it wrong all these years—and no, not only in Canada. It was originally spelled "shoo in." A racetrack term, it referred to a horse that had neither speed nor endurance, but would nevertheless win a race because the race was fixed. If the horse was having trouble making it over the finish line, there were people situated along the fence who were paid to "shoo" it across.

Perhaps I could make it to the Jeopardy semifinals, but only if shooers-in were allowed. A lot of my information, you see, is destined to disappear shortly, as it is floating around in a brain that has extremely fickle compartments and that does not offer an effective retrieval system unless, of course, the facts can attach themselves in passing to a receptive dendrite or two.

So, what can I say? Trivia is...well, trivial, which reminds me of at least one truism that emerged: The more you know, you more you realize how little you know. It was certainly true in my case. I was halfway through the manuscript before it occurred to me that I had no idea where the words "trivia" or "trivial" came from. I know now.

It all started in ancient Rome....

There were no newspapers, no televisions, and few people could read and write. If you were a merchant or a politician or someone who wanted to get the word out to people, what better place to stand than on a street corner? And if you got 20 visitors at a stall where two streets intersected, wouldn't it make sense that you would get even more at a corner where three streets intersected?

The significance of the three-road intersection was alluded to even earlier. Oedipus Rex was written in the fifth century BC by the Greek dramatist Sophocles. In the story, Oedipus (after whom the simple complex was named) made a life-determining decision at the fork of three roads:

"I will tell you all that happened there, my lady.
There were three highways
Coming together at a place that I passed...."

So it became a tradition that the smartest of the Roman merchants or politicians set up information stalls at corners where three streets intersected. And since most people had to commit the information to memory, only the barest of essential details were provided. You can see where this is going...three, in Latin, is "tri," and streets are "via." TRIVIA! But there's more.

In medieval times, the Latin liberal arts curriculum was divided into two major fields: the upper level or quadrivium, for older students, consisted of the four sciences (arithmetic, geometry, astronomy and music). The lower level or trivium, for beginning students, consisted of rhetoric, logic and grammar. Items that all beginning students were required to know, therefore, were called trivia.

Toward the end of the 16th century, the adjective "trivial" came into use to mean anything that was unimportant. Shakespeare, in *Henry VI, Part II,* is generally thought to be the first person to use the word "trivial" in its modern sense in literature.

Well, with that out of the way, there is little of substance left to write about the wild and wacky world of trivia—except that there's a lot more trivia out there. I suppose you could say there is absolutely no end to it. But I had to stop somewhere, and my publisher's word-length guideline was like the ribbon at the end of a marathon. With one last breath of stale, bookish air, I realized I'd crossed the finish line!

I enjoyed discovering little-known facts about this vast and varied country, many of which brought back sweet memories: warm summer nights at the drive-in, roadside attractions visited on cross-Canada family road trips and one fascinating dive I did at Lake Minnewanka in the mid-1970s with Dive Club pals from Calgary.

The statistics are as current as statistics can be—who knows how many more Canadians will drink a glass of beer by the time this book arrives in bookstores?— and every effort was made to give as clear and accurate a picture as possible of each item included herein. Even though the tone is light, I am aware that Canadians are, after all, serious in their wackiness, so no effort was spared to be truthful, above board and...well...Canadian about it all.

Enjoy!

ACROSS THE COUNTRY

This land is your land, this land is my land,
From Bonavista to Vancouver Island.

Words from the Canadian adaptation of Woody Guthrie's song "This Land Is Your Land,"
released in the 1960s by The Travellers, a Toronto folk group

Cross-Country Tour

Probably the best way to see this land of ours in all its diverse glory is to travel by car from one coast to the other. At just over 5500 kilometres in width and covering 9,970,610 square kilometres, Canada is the world's second-largest country (after Russia), occupying 7 percent of the Earth's land mass.

ABSOLUTELY CANADIAN   The Trans-Canada Highway is the longest national highway in the world. Stretching 7821 kilometres from Victoria, BC, to St. John's, NL, it was started in 1950 and officially opened on September 3, 1962. It took 20 years to complete the highway from coast to coast, and it cost an estimated $1 billion.

A Mari usque ad Mare

Canada's motto, "From sea to sea," is the Latin translation of a portion of Psalm 72:8, "He shall have dominion from sea to sea..."

Big Things to See

Canada is home to the world's largest collection (over 500 at last count) of oversize roadside attractions, many of which stand along the Trans-Canada Highway.

Eye-Popping!

From really big bites, like the huge perogy in Glendon, AB, or the big apple in Colborne, ON, to more esoteric giants, such as the flying saucer in Moonbeam, ON, or Noah's ark in Cobden, ON, you will be sure to get your eyeful of larger-than-life monuments. Monuments to what? you ask. That seems to be the big question.

Most of the giant monuments are whimsical, built to entertain. Others are tributes to local industry or resources:

- ☞ The Big Nickel was built in Sudbury, ON, in 1964 because Sudbury was the second-largest producer of nickel in the world.
- ☞ The Uranium Atom in Rolphton, ON, reflects the local leading role in Canada's nuclear industry.
- ☞ The oil derrick in Virden, MB, reminds people of the area's rich oil fields.

There are monuments to various forms of wildlife—fish, elk, moose, salmon, catfish, bears, dinosaurs, geese and sheep—and others to inanimate objects such as rocking chairs, fire hydrants, trucks, trains, pitchforks, canoes and carts, or clothing such as boots, hats and underwear. Some monuments even have names: Husky the Muskie (Kenora, ON), Chuck the Catfish (Selkirk, MB), Eddie the Squirrel (Edson, AB), Pemmican Pete (Regina, SK) and Klondike Mike (Edmonton AB).

Roadside Attractions

World's largest coke can—Portage la Prairie, MB

World's largest western boot—Edmonton, AB

World's largest tin soldier—New Westminster, BC

World's highest totem pole carved from a single tree—Victoria, BC

World's largest (fake) snowman—Beardmore, ON

World's largest beaver—Beaverlodge, AB

DID YOU KNOW?

The first road trip across Canada by car was made in 1912.

Span Ends an Era!

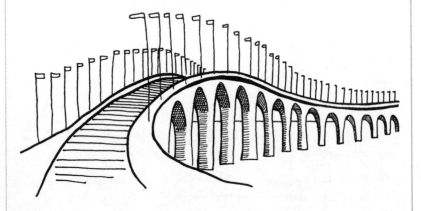

In spring 1997, the Confederation Bridge opened between Prince Edward Island and the mainland. Begun in 1993, the span provides a vital link between Islanders and the rest of Canada. There was joyous welcome for the bridge, but a sad farewell to an old lady.

On May 31, 1997, with three long blasts of her whistle, the icebreaking ferry boat *Abegweit II*, known affectionately as "The Old Lady of the Strait," said goodbye to a romantic era when she joined her sister ship, the original *Abegweit*, in retirement. The "Abbys" had been ferrying passengers and vehicles across the Northumberland Strait between the mainland and Prince Edward Island for 50 years, since August 14, 1947. Upon retirement,

Abegweit II became known as Club Ship *Abegweit*, to reflect her new role as clubhouse for the Columbia Yacht Club.

The Confederation Bridge is the world's longest uninterrupted span bridge. It crosses Northumberland Strait, connecting Borden-Carleton, PEI, and Journimain Island, NB, and consists of an 11- kilometre long main bridge span, with approach bridges for a total length of 12.9 kilometres. The bridge was completed on November 19, 1996, and over the next six months before the official opening in May 1997, workers installed traffic signals, emergency alarms, closed circuit televisions, and road- and weather-monitoring systems, and built a seven-lane toll plaza.

The world's longest street is Yonge Street in Toronto, ON. It is 1900 kilometres long and takes drivers all the way to Rainy River, ON.

Where Have All the Drive-Ins Gone?

- Remember those tinny speakers that used to hang on the car window?
- Remember your first kiss?
- Remember the animated ads for fresh popcorn and hot dogs that made your mouth water? And the announcement "Only five minutes left to showtime"?
- Remember Mom in her fluffy slippers, Dad in his comfortable flannel shirt and the kids in their PJs, all huddling in the heated privacy of the car, watching a family movie on the big screen?

Drive-in movies used to be BIG in Canada. By the late 1970s there were more than 300 drive-in theatres across Canada. Today, only 57 remain in operation.

Canada's first drive-in theatre opened on July 10, 1946, at Stoney Creek, ON, a town on the outskirts of Hamilton.

CITY POTPOURRI

What a Relief!

Spitting, urinating and defecating in public are against the law in Canada. Fines vary.

DID YOU  KNOW?

- ☞ The expression "neck of the woods," comes from the Algonquian word *naiak*, which means "a narrow strip of land in the woods."
- ☞ Hydro, as it refers to electricity produced from water power, is a uniquely Canadian word.

 Québec City is the only existing walled city in North America and the first city on this continent to be placed on UNESCO's World Heritage List.

Sounds Like the Taste Police...

In Kanata, ON, it is illegal to hang clothes in your backyard, and there are only certain colours you are permitted to use to paint the front door of your house or garage.

Our Own Atlantis

If anyone ever invites you to visit the town of Minnewanka Landing, be sure to take along a wetsuit. Lake Minnewanka, AB, is one of the most interesting towns in Canada—it is completely under water!

In the late 1800s, Minnewanka Landing was a pretty summer village on the lakeside, nestled in the mountains about 80 kilometres west of Calgary. It boasted hotels, restaurants, boardwalks, accessible public docks and two cruise boats that made daily tours.

In 1895, a decision was made to dam the lake in an attempt to improve the boggy shoreline to allow easier access for pleasure boaters. In 1912 the lake was again dammed, this time to provide hydroelectric power to nearby Calgary. A final dam was constructed in 1941, under the War Measures Act, to provide a source of power for Canada's war effort. The resulting rising water completely submerged the town.

Today, many of the original buildings remain, at depths ranging from approximately 12 metres to nearly 25 metres. Now part of Banff National Park, Minnewanka Landing Townsite is a fascinating destination for experienced SCUBA divers seeking the challenge of a cold water, high-altitude dive.

Same Old...Same Old

Some of the "temporary" government buildings erected on Carling Avenue, Sussex Drive and other locations in Ottawa during World War II were still in general and daily use some 50 years later.

Toronto's CN Tower is the tallest free-standing structure in the world. One of the Seven Wonders of the Modern World, it stands over 553 metres tall.

StatsCan

Seventy-nine percent of Canadians are urban dwellers.

Toronto, Montreal and Vancouver together are home to nearly one-third of Canada's population.

TAKING IT TO THE STREETS

Ho! Ho! Ho!

Santa Claus is the only individual in the world known to have his own postal code, H0H 0H0.

ABSOLUTELY
CANADIAN

Canada's Postal Codes

Canada's alphanumeric, six-character postal address system was introduced in 1971. The first three characters denote the FAS (forward sortation areas), with the first letter indicating the postal district, either the metropolitan area or geographic region. The second character, if zero, indicates a rural region; any other digit signifies an urban one. The third character further defines the specific area or section of the postal district.

The last three characters refer to the LDU (local delivery unit), which specifies a single address or range of addresses (such as an institution, office or apartment building). LDUs ending in zero indicate post office boxes.

That's a Lotta Mail!

There are currently approximately 840,000 postal codes in use in Canada. Not to worry. Even if the country's population expands a hundredfold, the alphanumeric combinations allow for a theoretical maximum of 7.2 million different codes.

DID YOU  KNOW?

- The LDU "9Z9" does not specify a location, but is used only for business reply mail.
- The letters D, F, I, O, Q and U are not used in postal codes because of their similarities to other letters and digits.

This Way to the Potlatch

We have our aboriginal ancestors to thank for road signs. Since the time before recorded history, First Nations people bent or twisted limbs of young, living trees situated at vital trail intersections to point the way for those who came after them.

If the trail marker needed to be permanent, the trail blazer would tie the twisted limbs with rawhide strips or wild vines. The twines broke as the tree grew, or rotted with the elements, but by that time the tree was already trained to grow in a certain position, pointing the way for the rest of its life.

World-Class Bridges

- The longest covered bridge in the world is the 391-metre bridge in Hartland, NB, built in 1901.
- The longest suspension bridge in Canada is the 668-metre Pierre Laporte Bridge in Quebec City, QC.
- The bridge with the longest uninterrupted span in the world is Confederation Bridge, opened in 1997. It spans the Northumberland Strait between New Brunswick and Prince Edward Island.

Fan Tan Alley in Victoria, BC, only 1.2 metres wide, is the narrowest street in the world. The site of numerous opium dens and gambling houses in the 1800s, during the early years of the city's Chinatown, the tiny street is named after Fan Tan, a popular Chinese game of chance.

Lighting the Way

Despite the discovery of electricity, the streets of many Canadian cities were still being lit by coal gas into the mid 1800s. Dirty, smelly and temperamental, coal gas lamps had to be regularly maintained by lamplighters hired to tend to them.

In 1883, Toronto was the first city in Canada to install electric street lights, followed closely by Victoria, also in 1883, then Calgary in 1890 and Edmonton in 1891.

AIR TRAVEL

Porno-Graphic? X-Rated Baggage on Air Canada

One large batch of Air Canada luggage security stickers, produced in 2004 by Canada's financially (and linguistically) challenged national airline, read:

THIS BAGGAGE HAS BEEN X-RATED AT POINT OF ORIGIN

Making Air Noises!

Poor command of written English aside, workers in Canada's major airlines have fallen far below passenger expectations according to reports from the soon-to-be-defunct (with the 2005 federal budget) Canadian Air Travel Complaints Commissioner's Office. One-third of the thousands of complaints were about customer service issues!

The first Canadian airport to receive designation as an international airport was Winnipeg Airport in 1928.

Winged Woman

Marion Alice Orr (1918–95), born in Toronto, ON, was the first Canadian woman to start her own flying school. Obtaining her private pilot's licence at the tender age of 22, Marion qualified for her commercial licence two years later. She worked for some time as an aircraft inspector with de Havilland Aircraft of Canada and became the second woman in Canada to qualify as an air traffic control assistant. In 1942 she was accepted into the Air Transport Auxiliary, where she logged 700 hours flying various types of aircraft, including the Spitfire. She opened her own airfield and flying school in Maple, ON, in 1949. Considered one of Canada's most distinguished pilots for her outstanding achievements in the field of aviation, Orr received, in 1976, a service medallion from the Ninety-Nines, an international organization of licensed women pilots, which once had Amelia Earhart as its president. Marion Orr was named to Canada's Aviation Hall of Fame in 1981.

Running on Empty

For safety reasons, jet planes are typically permitted to land at Canadian airports only when they have used up most of their fuel. To ensure compliance with the rule, flight crews keep extremely careful calculations of fuel consumption levels.

On August 10, 1949, A.V. Roe Canada's commercial jet, called the Avro Jetliner, was the first jet transport to fly in North America. The term "jetliner," which subsequently came into worldwide use, was coined by the company, but since the plane never went into production, Avro was unable to copyright the name. The Avro Jetliner was sold for scrap in 1956.

"Black Friday" and the End of an Era

The fighter jet known as the Avro Arrow was built for the cold war by A.V. Roe Canada. The first Avro Arrow, RL201, had its inaugural flight on March 25, 1958.

Deemed no longer necessary by John Diefenbaker's Conservative government, the project was axed on Friday, February 20, 1959. In a shocking announcement a short time later, the Department of Defence Production ordered the immediate destruction of all planes, prototypes, models, blueprints, pictures and film related to the Avro Arrow program. The last surviving Avro Arrow test pilot, Peter Cope, died of a heart attack on April 5, 2005, at the age of 85.

☞ On December 12, 1985, Canada experienced its worst air crash when an Arrow Airlines DC-8 crashed seconds after takeoff from a refuelling stop in Gander, NL, killing 248 members of the U.S. 101st Airborne Division and eight crew. Considered a weather-related crash, the disaster occurred shortly after freezing drizzle, blowing snow and a temperature of −42°C had been reported.

☞ The first death involving an airplane in Canada occurred on August 6, 1913. An American stunt pilot, John M. Bryant, was killed when his Curtiss seaplane crashed near Victoria, BC.

☞ The worst commercial airline accident in Canada involving Canadian aircraft occurred on November 29, 1963. A Trans-Canada Airlines DC-8F crashed four minutes after takeoff from Montréal International (now Trudeau) Airport, killing all 118 persons aboard.

☞ The average age of Air Canada pilots is 42 years. Retirement is compulsory at age 60.

Canada Hits the Skies!

John McCurdy was the first person in Canada to stay aloft in a heavier-than-air craft when he flew his Silver Dart over Bras d'Or Lake on Cape Breton Island on February 23, 1909.

Locations and codes of Canada's 10 busiest airports by passenger volume (2003 stats)

AIRPORT	CODE	CITY	PASS. VOL. (MILLIONS)
Pearson Int'l	YYZ	Toronto ON	23.0
Vancouver Int'l	YVR	Vancouver BC	13.2
Trudeau Int'l	YUL	Montreal QC	8.7
Mirabel Int'l	YMX	Montreal QC	
Calgary Int'l	YYC	Calgary AB	7.6
Edmonton Int'l	YEG	Edmonton AB	3.6
Macdonald-Cartier Int'l	YOW	Ottawa ON	3.1
Winnipeg Int'l	YWG	Winnipeg MB	2.7
Halifax Int'l	YHZ	Halifax NS	2.7
Greater Moncton Int'l	YQM	Moncton NB	0.4

Not So Busy After All...

Compare Canada's numbers to the world's busiest airport, Hartsfield International Airport in Atlanta, Georgia, which annually handles 77.9 million passengers!

DID YOU KNOW?

The Air Canada hangar at Toronto's Lester B. Pearson International Airport is equivalent in height to a seven-storey building.

In 2003, the online travel agency Expedia ranked Canadians among the worst tourists in the world, competing with Russians and Brits for the title of "rudest" by pushing their way to the front of lines, tipping poorly, complaining bitterly about everything from food to weather and refusing to speak local languages.

CANUCKS AND THEIR CARS

"The car has become an article of dress without which we feel uncertain, unclad and incomplete in the urban compound."

Marshall McLuhan (1911–80)

Ten-Year Casualty Rates on Canada's Roads

YEAR	# OF FATALITIES	# OF INJURIES (DOES NOT INCLUDE FATALITIES)
1993	3615	247,588
1994	3263	245,110
1995	3351	241,935
1996	3091	230,890
1997	3064	221,349
1998	2949	217,803
1999	2985	222,551
2000	2927	227,458
2001	2781	221,121
2002	2930	227,973
2003	2778	222,260

In 2003, over 60 percent of all drivers who died as the result of vehicle accidents were between 20 and 34 years of age (29.1 percent aged 20 to 24 and 31 percent aged 25 to 34). The 35–44 age group was close behind at 28.5 percent.

DID YOU KNOW?

Approximately 25 percent of the vehicles stolen in Canada are never recovered.

The highest rates of vehicle theft in Canada have consistently been reported from Manitoba. In 2001 alone there were 1148 thefts per 100,000 population—more than double the national average.

Hmmm...Where to Park in the Morning?

Theft Occurrences, Time:
Most vehicle thefts occur
between 6 AM and noon.
Theft Occurences, Place:
40 percent in parking lots
30 percent on the street
16 percent in private
driveways or
garages

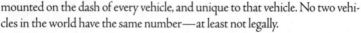

Identity Theft!

For those of you who treat
your vehicles like lovers,
you'll be happy to know
that every car has an
identifying mark, almost as
individual as a human finger-
print. It is the vehicle ID number,
engraved on the small metal tag

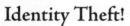

mounted on the dash of every vehicle, and unique to that vehicle. No two vehicles in the world have the same number—at least not legally.

However, car theft rings have begun to use a procedure police refer to as "cloning." Thieves steal a car, then find another of similar description in a parking lot, on the street or in an auto wrecking yard. Using the second car's unique ID number, they create a counterfeit tag, which they place on their hot vehicle. The newly ID'd vehicle now cannot be traced back to the rightful owner and can be registered and sold in another province or country.

Way To Go, Canada!

Thanks to increased driver savvy, stiffer penalties and DD (designated driver) programs, this country's impaired driving rate continues on a 20-year decline.

Hate To Say It, But We Win Again!
In 2000, Canada's car theft rate was 26 percent higher than our American neighbour's.

Up, Up and Away!
☞ The vehicle theft rate has been increasing annually since 2000.
☞ In 2003 alone, 171,017 vehicles were stolen in Canada.

A Hummer-Dinger!
An enterprising thief may have thought he would score some points towards entry through the Golden Gates recently when he bought and insured a new Hummer with a $100,000 illegally acquired bank loan. He then shipped the car off to Poland for delivery to a high-ranking church cleric. The police intervened when the original owner reported the Hummer stolen and tried to claim the insurance.

☞ The number of motor vehicles in Canada has more than doubled since 1970 and is currently growing faster than the Canadian population!

☞ With an average of .58 vehicles per person, Canada has the fourth-highest vehicle per capita rate in the world, after only the United States, Luxembourg and Australia. That figure works out to more than one car for every two Canadians of all ages.

DID YOU KNOW?

Fifteen seconds of idling a car uses more fuel than restarting it!

I'd Drive a Mile for a Deal
Car-obsessed Canadians have proven to be just as obsessed with spiralling gas prices. In a 2004 study sponsored by General Motors Canada, 92 percent of Canadian drivers reported being willing to drive out of their way for a $0.20/litre gas discount. To get that discount, 10 percent of drivers were willing to drive for an extra 30 minutes, and 50 percent would wait in line for 10 minutes or more (one hopes they'd wait with their engines off).

The Pits
A visitor to Niagara Falls reported that his vehicle had just been stolen, but the police didn't believe his story. Two months earlier, the car was impounded by police when they found it abandoned in a gravel pit. The owner had abandoned it there himself, hoping to claim the insurance and buy a new car.

FULL FATHOM FIVE

The legend lives on, from the Chippewa on down
of the big lake they call Gitche Gumee.
The lake, it is said, never gives up her dead
when the skies of November turn gloomy.

Gordon Lightfoot (1938–)

from "The Wreck of the *Edmund Fitzgerald*"

The Pride of the American Side

The *Edmund Fitzgerald*, at 729 feet long, 75 feet wide and weighing over 13,000 tons, was the largest ship to sail the Great Lakes when she was launched in 1958, but even she was no match for the Great Gitche Gumee. The great ship left port at Superior, WI, on November 9, 1975, heading for Detroit. On board were 26,000 tons of iron ore pellets and a crew of 29 men. They never made it.

A severe storm hit, with five-metre waves and winds in excess of 100 km/hour. The last signal was received on the Canadian side at 7:25 PM on November 10. All on board were lost when the *Edmund Fitzgerald* sank to the bottom.

When the Skies of November Turn Gloomy

- ☞ The *Daniel J. Morrell* sank in Lake Huron on November 29, 1966, killing 28 crew.
- ☞ The *Carl D. Bradley* sank in Lake Michigan on November 18, 1958, killing 33 men.
- ☞ Three freighters went down and 57 crew members were lost on Lake Michigan during a period of intense storms between November 11 and 13 in 1940. (Although no part of Lake Michigan lies in Canada, there were a number of Canadian crew members aboard the U.S. ships that went down).
- ☞ The most recent total loss in Lake Superior was the U.S. Coast Guard Vessel *Mesquite*. It did not sink in November, but close—on December 4, 1989.

The Great Lake they call K-Che-Gu-Mme

With an average depth of 147 metres, and some areas reaching 405 metres, Lake Superior is well named. The Algonquin called the lake K-Che-Gu-Mme (anglicized as Gitche-Gumee), meaning "all-powerful lake." Waves in Lake Superior can grow even higher than those found in the ocean due to wind fetches* reaching up to 500 kilometres along its 563-kilometre length. The oldest fossils found anywhere, Stromatolites, have been found in the rocks along Whitefish Bay, giving proof of life in that region over one and a half billion years ago.

Wrecks of the Great Lakes

LAKE	# OF KNOWN WRECKS
Lake Erie	1900
Lake Huron	1400
Lake Michigan	2500
Lake Ontario	1200
Lake Superior	700

Major Shipwrecks in Canadian Waters

PROVINCE	# OF KNOWN WRECKS
Newfoundland	7000
Prince Edward Island	700
Nova Scotia	9600
New Brunswick	1800
Québec	3800
Ontario	4100
British Columbia	3600

DID YOU  KNOW?

Pelee Passage, a 20-kilometre stretch of water between Pelee Island and Point Pelee, ON, is one of the most treacherous passages in Lake Erie, having claimed more than 200 ships since the early 1800s.

* Wind fetch: The distance of open water over which the wind blows. The larger the fetch, the larger the waves.

Historical Canadian Casualties
on the Great Lakes

(Note the number of wrecks that occurred in November)

September 17, 1949. *Noronic*, liner, caught fire on Lake Ontario

September 24, 1947. *Milverton*, freighter, caught fire on Lake Ontario

December 8, 1927. *Kamloops*, freighter, sank in Lake Huron

November 9, 1913. *Leafield*, freighter, missing in storm on Lake Huron

November 9, 1913. *Regina*, freighter, missing in storm on Lake Huron

November 8, 1913. *James C. Carruthers*, freighter, missing in storm on Lake Ontario

November 8, 1913. *Wexford*, freighter, missing in storm on Lake Huron

September 9, 1889. *Rothesay*, paddlewheeler, sank in collision on Lake Ontario

May 30, 1888. *Maggie Mcrae*, freighter, foundered in ice on Lake Superior

November 7, 1885. *Algoma*, steamer, stranded in storm on Lake Huron

July 25, 1877. *Cumberland*, paddlewheeler, stranded on Lake Superior

August 12, 1865. *Pewabic*, freighter, sank in collision on Lake Superior

The *San Juan*, submerged in Red Bay in the Strait of Belle Isle, is the oldest and most complete 16th-century transatlantic merchant shipwreck known.

AURORA BOREALIS

The Northern Lights have seen queer sights,
But the queerest they ever did see
Was the night on the marge of Lake Labarge
I cremated Sam McGee.

Robert W. Service (1874–1958)
from "The Cremation of Sam McGee"

What Are the Aurora Borealis?

These breathtaking displays of northern lights originate on the sun, where explosions and flares occur at frequent intervals. During explosions, large quantities of solar debris are hurled into space as plasma clouds at speeds 1000 of km/second. As the clouds near Earth, they are attracted by the magnetic fields at the Earth's poles. The lights we see are the visible effects of light particles (photons) produced when the solar particles collide with gases in Earth's atmosphere.

Picture This!

About 100 million photons are needed to produce a light bright enough to be seen by the naked eye. The strongest northern lights are equal in brightness to the moon.

Colour

Unlike the sun, the aurora does not produce all colours in the spectrum. Different colours are produced by the various gases in the aurora:

Yellow-green—Oxygen

Red—High-altitude oxygen

Blue—Ionized nitrogen

Violet—Neutral nitrogen

In most regions of Canada, the northern lights usually appear yellow-green, but on rare occasions, brilliant red or violet northern lights may appear in the sky during periods of extreme solar disturbance.

Shape

Typically seen in arcs, rays, bands and curtains, auroras can move in very slow, undulating waves or, during periods of high solar activity, in flashing and rapidly changing patterns.

Why Aurora Borealis?

The origin of the name "aurora borealis" is under some dispute. Galileo Galilei, a 16th-century Italian scientist, and Pierre Gassendi, a French astronomer, have both been credited with naming the phenomenon after Aurora, the Roman goddess of the dawn, and Boreas, the Roman god of the north wind. Before the 16th century, the lights were referred to in Italy and France as "red dawn of the North." It was not a coincidence: both countries lie at latitudes where the northern lights appear red.

The most brilliant displays of northern lights are seen

- on clear nights
- in winter
- from one to two hours before to one to two hours after midnight
- in years of major sunspot activity (about every 12 years)
- when the sun's active areas face Earth (every 27 days)

DID YOU KNOW?

Although the northern lights are occasionally visible in Canada, there are better places in the world from which to see them:

- Norway—almost every clear, dark night
- Alaska—five to ten times a month
- Northern British Isles—roughly once a month
- Northern Canada—two to four times a year

And worse places:

- Mexico and Mediterranean countries—Once or twice per decade
- Equatorial regions—Once in 200 years

The Canadian Space Agency and NASA have set up a joint endeavour to study the northern lights in an attempt to gain a better understanding about when they will occur. In addition to emitting light, the aurora releases energy that distorts magnetic fields, causing damage to communication satellites above the Earth and creating power surges on the ground, which in turn result in electrical outages and damage to electronic equipment.

If scientists can predict when a solar wind is about to occur, there can be temporary load reductions on Earth-bound power grids that may lessen the impact of power surges on our electrical systems, thus preventing power outages.

DID YOU  KNOW?

Predictions and reports on near-space phenomena are collectively known as "space weather." Although considerably less accurate than meteorological reports for Earth, they may give aurora hunters an idea of when to watch for super displays.

Is it aroma faint from Nature's chalice,
The odour of the aurora borealis
That shifts before the stars a silver fume,
Or peacock-tints on pools of amber gloom
In some fur-forest, all of light deluded,
With the vain thought that here it lived before
In many incarnations o'er and o'er,
Till all this life seems but a spectral show
Of something real that perished long ago?

Duncan Campbell Scott (1862–1947)
from "Reverie"

Duncan Campbell Scott, along with Archibald Lampman and Bliss Carmen, was considered one of Canada's Confederation poets. Born in Ottawa in 1862, Scott was primarily known for his work with the federal government's Department of Indian Affairs. His poetry, which was first published when Scott was 31 years old, showed the collision between white society and aboriginal people, whose culture was being forever altered by his department's policies.

The Stuff of Legends

The light displays encouraged ancient peoples in the north to come up with explanations for their sudden and often terrifying appearance:

- Many northern peoples believed the aurora was the medium through which the dead could contact living relatives.
- Lakota Sioux believed the lights were spirits of children yet unborn.
- Children in many northern communities are warned not to whistle or shout at the northern lights for fear they will come to take them away or, as some Inuit art depicts, to decapitate them.
- The Vikings believed the lights were reflections of dead maidens.
- The Japanese believed the lights would favour any child conceived under them.
- In Danish folklore, the lights were a flock of swans, frantically trying to free themselves after being trapped in ice.

Do You Hear What I Hear?

Although many people claim to have heard the northern lights, the question of whether or not they produce sound is still unanswered, despite many attempts to investigate it.

Curative Powers

The light from the aurora borealis was, even until recent times, considered by some Inuit tribes to have curative powers. Sick people were often taken outdoors during a display to be cured, and healers made spirit journeys into the lights to obtain advice.

AVALANCHE!
Clear and Ever-Present Danger

In the past 20 years there have been over 200 deaths resulting from avalanches in Canada. Since 1800, avalanches have killed more than 600 people in Canada. The majority of cases occur in British Columbia and Alberta, with a few each year in Québec. The current national average is about 14 deaths per year— comparatively low when compared to the numbers in the United States and France. (See table below.)

YEAR	CANADA	UNITED STATES	FRANCE
1985–1986	4	17	40
1986–1987	7	21	24
1987–1988	7	8	24
1988–1989	6	6	17
1989–1990	9	8	28
1990–1991	11	8	47
1991–1992	2	24	No records
1992–1993	9	29	23
1993–1994	8	13	23
1994–1995	15	28	23
1995–1996	9	30	43
1996–1997	14	22	23
1997–1998	23	26	35
1998–1999	17	32	44
1999–2000	10	22	26
2000–2001	12	33	30
2001–2002	13	35	29
2002–2003	29	58	26
2003–2004	11	34	29
2004–2005	7	27	25
Totals	223	481	559

Major Avalanche Disasters in Canada in the Last 50 Years

1955   Mount Temple, Lake Louise, AB—seven skiers killed

1965   Granduc Mining Camp, BC—26 miners dead, 22 injured

1971   Terrace, BC—seven dead, one survivor when a café was hit by an avalanche

1979   Purcell Range southwest of Golden, BC—seven heli-skiers killed

1981   Near Conrad Icefield, west of Golden, BC—three heli-skiers killed

1987   Near Blue River, BC—six heli-skiers and their guide killed

1990   Banff National Park, AB—four people killed while cross-country skiing

1991   Bugaboo Glacier Provincial Park, BC—nine heli-skiers killed

1999   Inuit community of Kangiqsualujjuaq, QC—25 injured and 9 dead, including 5 children, when an avalanche destroyed the school gymnasium

2003   29 dead as a result of avalanches. The list of casualties included one snowshoer who was killed in Alberta. The remainder were snowmobilers and skiers with little or no experience, all killed in BC.

How Does an Avalanche Occur?

Avalanches are mass downhill movements of snow and ice. Critical combinations of topographical or climatic conditions appear to be common features of many avalanche incidents.

Weather conditions that contribute to avalanches:

- Heavy precipitation (rain or snow, but especially rain)
- Strong wind
- Rapidly rising temperatures

Terrain conditions that contribute to avalanches:

- 30° to 40° degree slopes (though they may occur on slopes anywhere between 25° and 50°), typically at a convex section
- Slopes above or near the treeline
- Slopes with rocky ground cover
- Leeward-facing slopes (slopes facing away from where the wind blows)

Canadian Avalanche Warning Scale

DANGER LEVEL	COLOUR	PROBABILITY AND TRIGGER	RECOMMENDED ACTION
Low	Green	Natural avalanches very unlikely Human-triggered avalanches very unlikely	Travel generally safe Normal caution advised
Moderate	Yellow	Natural avalanches unlikely Human-triggered avalanches possible	Use caution in steeper terrain on certain aspects
Considerable	Amber	Natural avalanches possible Human-triggered avalanches probable	Be increasingly cautious on steeper terrain
High	Red	Natural and human-triggered avalanches likely	Travel in avalanche terrain not recommended
Extreme	Deep Red	Widespread natural or human-triggered avalanches certain	Travel in avalanche terrain should be avoided and confined to low angle terrain, well away from avalanche path run-outs

Note: In February 2005, Parks Canada in association with the Canadian Avalanche Association announced the implementation of a new icon-based public avalanche warning system, which will present colour-coded icons (red—high risk, yellow—medium risk, and green—low risk) representing general avalanche risk within forecast regions.

Canada's Son
Michel Trudeau, 23-year-old son of the late Pierre Elliott Trudeau, was on a backcountry ski trip when he was swept into Lake Kokanee by an avalanche on November 13, 1998. His body was never recovered.

DID YOU KNOW?

☞ Precipitation (snow and rain) is the most common weather-related cause of avalanches. Wind is the second most common cause.
☞ You may be able to survive an avalanche in motion by "swimming" upwards through the snow. Once the avalanche comes to a stop, if you are unsure which way is up, make a small space around your face and spit. The saliva will fall downhill, and you might be able to dig in the opposite direction to fresh air.

CLIMATIC CONDITIONS

Mon pays ce n'est pas un pays, c'est l'hiver
Mon jardin ce n'est pas un jardin, c'est la plaine
Mon chemin ce n'est pas un chemin, c'est la neige
Mon pays ce n'est pas un pays, c'est l'hiver

Gilles Vigneault (1928–)
from "Mon pays"

Québec's celebrated singer, who wrote the words and music to the song many hailed as Québec's unofficial anthem, may have overstated the conditions somewhat:

"My country is not a country, it is winter;
My garden is not a garden, it is the prairie;
My road is not a road, it is the snow;
My country is not a country, it is winter."

Warm Feet, Cold Head

Most of Canada lies in the north temperate zone, but the country's vastness creates an amazing variety of local climates. From the perpetually frozen Arctic regions to the parched desert-like areas of the Cypress Hills to the grape-growing wine regions of southern Ontario, Canada boasts one of the most varied climates in the world.

Yeah, Annie!

Prince Edward Island is the only province in Canada that has never experienced temperatures below –40°C.

Chalk This One Up!

On September 8, 1954, Canadians welcomed television into their homes. The first person to appear onscreen was Percy Saltzman, a meteorologist and Canada's first TV weather reporter. For the next 22 years he ended his weather report with a toss of his chalk and a chirpy "And that's the weather!"

Earthquakes, Tsunamis and Floods...Oh my!

Yes, Canada has them all. We also have our share of drought, cyclones, hurricanes, tornadoes—even typhoons!

JUNE 30, 1912: A tornado ripped through a section of Regina, SK. Lasting only three minutes, it killed 40 people, injured 300 and left 25 percent of the population homeless.

NOVEMBER 18, 1929: An earthquake in the Grand Banks off Newfoundland's Burin Peninsula measured 7.2 on the Richter scale. It was followed two-and-a-half hours later by a massive 27-metre tsunami that crashed to shore, killing 29 people, sweeping homes and boats out to sea and destroying nearly 50 kilometres of coastline.

OCTOBER 15, 1954: Hurricane Hazel hit the north shore of Lake Ontario, dumping 300 million tonnes of rain on Toronto and killing 83 people. Some of the bodies were not found until almost a week later, when they washed ashore in New York State.

SUMMER 1961: Drought in the southern Prairies caused losses in wheat production that amounted to close to $700 million. A one-year drought of equal severity that began in late summer 1987 created such a disaster across the southern Prairies that 10 percent of farmers left agriculture. Recovery costs amounted to $4 billion.

OCTOBER 12, 1962: Typhoon Freda struck British Columbia's Lower Mainland and the southern portion of Vancouver Island, destroying nearly one-quarter of Vancouver's Stanley Park and causing winds to gust to 145 km/h. Seven deaths were reported.

SEPTEMBER 7, 1991: A severe hailstorm in Calgary pelted houses with 10-centimetre hailstones. Trees, roofs, windows and automobiles were destroyed in the 30-minute barrage that left damages in excess of $300 million.

MARCH 15, 1993: A cyclone off the coast of Nova Scotia produced waves over 30 metres high. An oceangoing vessel, the *Gold Bond Conveyer*, capsized and sank, killing 33 crew members.

Groundhog Predictions

Wiarton Willie is a real live groundhog who lives on Brown Street in Wiarton, ON. Every February, little Willie steps outside to predict the coming of spring. If he sees his shadow, he goes back inside, telling us there will be another six weeks of winter. Wiarton Willie and his predecessors have been predicting the coming of spring in Canada since 1956. It is said that their predictions are as good as those made by meteorologists—accurate about 25 percent of the time!

DID YOU  KNOW?

- ☞ Rain is measured in millimetres (mm) and snow in centimetres (cm). To measure total precipitation, convert snow to mm and add it to the rain total.
- ☞ Lowest recorded temperature: –63°C in Snag, YT (February 3, 1947)
- ☞ Highest recorded temperature: 45°C in Midale, SK (July 5, 1937)

SNOW

Let It Snow!

Canada's love affair with snow is natural. For often more than half the year, most of Canada is covered in the white stuff.

A Hundred Words for Snow

Although we often hear that the Inuit of northern Canada have over a hundred words for snow, this is a stretch of the truth. Lexicologists (word experts) estimate that the Inuit have no more words for snow than we do, but that they have many different word forms (lexemes) used to describe snow.

THINGS YOU CAN DO WITH SNOW	THINGS YOU CAN MAKE WITH SNOW
Snowshoeing	Snowman
Sledding/tobogganing	Snowballs
Skiing	Snow fort
Snowboarding	Snow angels
Snow shovelling	Maple syrup toffee
Snow blowing	Snow cones
Snowmobiling	

Canada's largest snowman (15.6 metres high) was built in Winnipeg in February 1988. It sported the world's largest toque: 43 metres long and 4.9 metres in diameter!

Dig It?

In February 1948, a farmer from Moose Jaw, SK, had to chop through the roof of his barn to feed his cows following a massive snowstorm. In some prairie towns, snowdrifts reached the tops of telephone poles.

Quiz Question

How many English words do you know for snow? (HINT: Ask a skier!)

Possible answers: Sleet, slush, powder, corn, fluff, sugar, whiteout, boilerplate, crystals, crust, hardpack, drift, flake, pellets, graupel, windpack, blizzard, avalanche

Regardless of their size, shape or weight, snowflakes fall at 5 km/h.

Canada's Worst Blizzards

NEWFOUNDLAND: On February 16, 1959, there were five-metre drifts and 70,000 people without power.

SOUTHERN PRAIRIES: On December 15, 1964, there were 90 km/h winds, –34°C temperatures and three fatalities.

SOUTHERN MANITOBA: On March 4 and 5, 1966, there were 35 centimetres of snow and 120 km/h winds.

MONTRÉAL, QC: On November 7 and 8, 1969, there were 70 centimetres of snow and 15 fatalities, while from March 4 to 11, 1971, there were 47 centimetres of snow and 110 km/h winds.

LONDON, ON: From December 9 to 12, 1977, 100 centimetres of snow fell.

 Bombardier, the Québec company that invented the snowmobile, also designed and built monorails for Walt Disney World. The company also built trains for the Chunnel between Britain and France, and subway trains for New York City.

Other Snow-Related Items Invented by Canadians
Snow blower
Ski bindings
Rotary snow plough

Snow goggles were invented by the Inuit. They were built for protection from niphablepsia (snow blindness).

- At 340 centimetres, Québec City has Canada's deepest average annual lasting snow coverage.
- The Canadian record for greatest snowfall in one day was 145 centimetres, recorded in Tahtsa Lake, BC, on February 11, 1999.
- Lowest average annual snowfall in Canada is 47 centimetres in Victoria, BC.
- Most days with blowing snow is 37 days per year in Chicoutimi, QC.

What a Dump!

On March 4, 1971, Montréal city workers hauled away 500,000 truckloads of snow after 47 centimetres were dumped on the city during its worst snowstorm. Seventeen people died, and winds up to 110 km/h created drifts that reached to second-storey windows.

Inukshuk

Helping travellers find their way on the snow-covered expanses of the North is one of the many uses for these stone structures made by the Inuit. *Inukshuk* (also spelled *Inuksuk*) means "that which acts on behalf of man" in Inuktitut. Made of stones balanced upon one another in the shape of a human form, these figures can be almost any size, from small enough to hold in your hand to nearly life-size. They are still used in the Arctic to show direction, to indicate migration paths of caribou or to warn of danger. Destruction of an Inukshuk is forbidden in Inuit tradition.

The 2010 Winter Olympic Games, to be held in Vancouver, BC, will feature a stylized Inukshuk called Oly as its logo.

Snow Joke!

In Kanata, ON, it is illegal to shovel snow from your driveway onto your lawn or onto the street. So... where do they put it?

Snowy Place Names

Over 200 place names in Canada feature the word "snow," and every province (except for PEI*) has at least one place name containing the word "snow."

Enough To Go Around!

During the Winter Olympic Games in Lake Placid, NY, in 1932, a stretch of mild weather melted the snow on cross-country ski trails. Truckloads of snow were brought in from Canada to save the event!

The Lorch Snowplane

In 1929, Karl E. Lorch, an inventive Saskatchewan man from Spy Hill, developed a marvellous contraption using a Ford engine, a makeshift sled and an airplane propellor. He assembled these parts into a vehicle that could transport people across the snow-covered prairies where no roads existed. By the late 1930s, Lorch's ever-evolving vehicles were being used by mail carriers in North Dakota and rural medical doctors on the Canadian prairies.

Canada's Snowbird Triplets

SNOWBIRD #1—The Canadian Forces' synchronized aerobatic flying elite, who, since 1970, have been flying in precision formation in the skies, demonstrating the skill, professionalism and teamwork of the men and women of our military.

SNOWBIRD #2—Canada's unfettered and unfeathered citizens (typically seniors) who fly or drive south to escape the ravages of a Canadian winter.

SNOWBIRD #3—Nova Scotia's school-teaching songstress Anne Murray (born June 20, 1945), who became an almost instant success with her award-winning song "Snowbird" in 1969, becoming the first Canadian solo female to earn American gold record status.

Florida's the Fave!

In 2003 alone, Canadians collectively spent 69,429 days in U.S. cities. More than half of that time (57 percent) was spent in warm-weather areas: 45.7 percent in Florida and 11.3 percent in California!

---

* Okay, so PEI doesn't have a place name with snow in it. But we can forgive them. They provide us with the delicacy known as snow crab!

WATER, WATER EVERYWHERE!

Rub-A-Dub-Dub, Canucks in a Tub!

It all started with Canada's 100th birthday, when Nanaimo citizen Glen Galloway came up with an idea for a great celebration race from Nanaimo across the Strait of Georgia to English Bay in Vancouver. Frank Ney, a member of the Centennial Celebrations Committee (and future mayor of Nanaimo) promoted the idea. The first race was held in centennial year, 1967, with 212 entries.

Eighty of the floating tubs never made it out of the harbour that first year, and only 50 got to the finish line. But a Canadian event was born and has been gaining followers every year. Running under the auspices of the Loyal Nanaimo Bathtub Society, the annual bathtub run now signs in entries that number in the thousands.

Regardless of how formal the event pretends to be, it is still a riot of crazy activity and shows just how funny and inventive Canadians can be. In the early 1990s, *Time* magazine published an article on the race: "Rub-A-Dub-Dub, Nuts in a Tub." Shortly after the story hit the headlines, bathtub race organizers decided to allow foreign participation, likely to prove once and for all that Canadians are not the only nutty people on the planet.

A Rather Shallow Rule

In Etobicoke, ON, residents must bathe with no more than nine centimetres of water in the bathtub!

Down-unders Refuse to Sink to Our Depths!

International competitors have been in the lineup since 1996, when Nanaimo hosted the World International Bathtub Championships, and those wild and crazy Australians have been dominating the world's cleanest sport in recent years.

An Idea that Does Hold Water

So will a vessel originally intended to hold water actually float?
The answer is, quite simply, yes.

AND NO. Although the long list of rules (28 at last count) keeps the playing field, er...water... relatively calm, the definition of "bathtub" has evolved over the years. Vessels need not be actual bathtubs from your home or someone else's, but they must "convey the impression of a bathtub." That said, they must conform to the size and shape of a recognizable roll-edge bathtub, have a minimum weight of 160 kilograms with driver, and be powered by fuel available to the general public (e.g., no rocket fuel allowed!).

Where Has All the Water Gone?

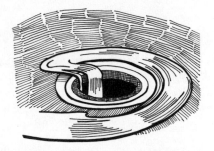

- ☛ Flushing the toilet uses 15 to 19 litres
- ☛ The average shower uses 100 litres
- ☛ Dishwashers use 40 litres
- ☛ Brushing teeth with tap running uses 10 litres
- ☛ Automatic washing machine uses 225 litres
- ☛ Tub baths (except in Etobicoke) use 60 litres

ABSOLUTELY CANADIAN

Drawings, drawings everywhere, and hers went on with ink! The *Guinness Book of World Records* co-title-holder for World's Most Tattooed Woman happens to be a Canadian stripper and dancer, Krystyne Kolorful, who has an entire body suit of ink markings amassed over a 10-year period. Even if Krystyne had access to all the water in Canada, she would not be able to wash them off.

DID YOU KNOW?

A single lawn sprinkler spraying 20 litres per minute uses more water in one hour than all of the following combined:

☞ ten toilet flushes
☞ two dishwasher loads
☞ two five-minute showers
☞ one washer-load of laundry

Speaking of Bathtubs...

British Columbia is the official bathtub racing capital of the world!

CANADA'S LARGEST LAKES (IN SQUARE KILOMETRES)

Superior (ON)	84,500*
Huron (ON)	63,500*
Great Bear (NT/YT)	31,400
Great Slave (NT)	28,400
Erie (ON)	25,800*
Winnipeg (MB)	24,400
Ontario (ON)	19,300*
Athabasca (AB/SK)	7940
Reindeer (SK)	6640
Nettiling (NT)	5530
Winnipegosis (MB)	5360
Nipigon (ON)	4850
Manitoba (MB)	4630
Lake of the Woods (ON)	4340*
Dubawnt (NT)	3830

* Includes area extending into the United States

ICE

In the land of the pale blue snow, where it's ninety-nine below
And the polar bears are dancing o'er the plain,
In the shadow of the pole, I'll clasp her to my soul
To be married when the ice worms nest again.

Attributed to Robert W. Service (1874–1958)
from "When the Ice Worms Nest Again"

Ice Worms

Legends of the Tuchone people of southern Yukon describe giant ice worms that emerge from the glaciers of the St. Elias Mountains when the Midnight Sun disappears from the sky. They feast on people, leaving behind a shell of greyish, dead skin. An Inuit myth refers to Sikusi, a mischievous ice worm.

The legends inspired an inside joke for bartenders and seasoned prospectors during the Klondike Gold Rush. They created a drink called the "ice-worm cocktail," which they gave to tenderfoot prospectors as a rite of passage. The "worm" was actually a piece of flaccid, cooked spaghetti, suspended in alcohol. The drink reduced the number of prospectors who stayed to fight over claims.

WARNING
Be sure to check your next drink.

The Worm Turns

You may not want to know this, but ice worms really exist. In fact, three creatures known as ice worms live in the frozen north:

- A dark-pigmented, smooth worm (*Mesenchytraeus solifugus*) found in tangled masses in melting glacier ice
- A fuzzy caterpillar (*Gynaephora lepidoptera*) that is tolerant of frigid conditions
- A wingless, creamy white insect (*Grylloblatta campodeiformis*) found at the edges of melting glaciers

Icebreakers

Canada has had icebreakers for over 100 years, with its first icebreaking ferries in operation between Prince Edward Island and the mainland as early as 1876. Today, Canada operates 22 of the world's 100 icebreakers.

Breaking the Ice!

It's called the Amphibex, and it is manufactured in Terrebonne, QC. The large, citrus yellow, amphibious icebreaker is being used with great success on the St. Lawrence River, breaking up ice before ice jams form and removing ice once jams occur.

Price tag: $460,000 pre-owned.

First Skaters

According to legend, the Iroquois attached shin bones of animals to their footwear with leather thongs in order to travel across frozen bodies of water.

 John Forbes, of Dartmouth, NS, designed the first spring skate in 1861. It used a single lever, rather than the traditional screws and plates, to attach the blade to the wearer's boots.

 Ottawa's Rideau Canal, at 7.8 kilometres, is the longest outdoor skating rink in the world.

The Wacky Canuck Sport of Hard-Water Fishing

Particularly well-known for minus double-digit cold weather and hardy citizens, Canada is also home to the largest number of people who engage in the weird and wonderful sport of hard-water fishing. Otherwise known as ice fishing, this activity has been around for centuries.

Traditionally practised as a subsistence activity by aboriginal peoples, ice fishing has become an increasingly popular pastime. In Québec's Saguenay region, there were 1600 huts moved onto a frozen fiord during the four-month winter fishing season in 2003.

What's in a Name?
West Pubnico, a small fishing village on Nova Scotia's south shore, derived its name from the Mi'kmaq word *Pombcoup,* meaning, "a hole that has been cut into the ice for fishing."

DID YOU KNOW?

In 2000 alone, Canadian anglers spent a combined total of 4,489,296 days fishing through ice!

No Fishing on Thin Ice

Ice thickness of 10 centimetres is recommended for individual angling; 18 centimetres for groups; 28 centimetres if you want to drive your truck up to the door of your luxury hut.

Roughing It—Not!

Many ice-fishing huts offer all the comforts of home: wooden plank floors, portable heaters, discarded kitchen tables and chairs and hand-me-down sofas (or, to use the Canuck term, chesterfields). Some even have pictures on the walls, curtains in the windows, portable television sets, stereos and camp cots for that afternoon snooze when the fish are napping.

Here's a Little Tip-Up

With all the distractions present in an ice-fishing hut (card playing, beer drinking, TV watching), it's no surprise that persistent hard-water anglers have had to design a unique tool. A wood-and-metal device reminiscent of the dipping-head drinking ducks that used to be popular in bars, the tip-up (*brimbale* in French) alerts an otherwise occupied angler that a fish is nibbling the line. A battery-operated device is now available that will monitor activity on a tip-up from a remote location. With tricks like this, hard-water fishermen don't even have to show up!

Pass the Bologna!

Fewer than one-third of the fish caught from beneath the ice are eaten. More than 60 percent are caught and released.

DID YOU KNOW?

As water near the surface of a lake cools, it becomes heavier and sinks, pushing warmer water to the surface, where it too is cooled. Before ice can form on a lake surface, the entire column of water must cool to 4°C. Then it can begin to cool to the 0° required for total surface freezing. Because of the additional effect of turbulence, the entire water column must reach 0° before freezing can begin in rivers.

- The first covered skating rink in the world was built in Québec City in 1852.
- Victoria Skating Rink, built in Montréal in 1862, was for several years the largest skating rink in the world.

Double-Barrelled Effort
John Munday, a Canadian mechanic, made two successful Niagara plunges in a barrel. The first was on October 5, 1985; the second on September 26, 1993.

By the Way...
Leave your cello at home when you visit Niagara Parks. It is illegal to play any instrument in public within park boundaries.

Now Here's a Fishy Story!
A few years ago, a tourist walking along the boardwalk near Cave of the Winds at Niagara Falls was minding his own business when an airborne salmon hit him in the face. The salmon was attempting to make its way down the falls to the pools below when it got a little too exuberant. The fish ended up as dinner for the man and his family.

(Fishy Factoid: Yes, fish regularly take the plunge over the falls to the pools below without harm to life or fin.)

 Canada's Manitou Lake on Manitoulin Island (Lake Huron), is the world's largest lake on an island in a lake.

Clearly un-Canadian
The zebra mussel is an invasive foreign species believed to have been transported in the ballast water of ships arriving in Canada from Europe. First discovered in 1988, the mussels have brought one positive effect for Lake Ontario's diving industry: the water is clearer than ever before. Sadly, they are slowly but surely killing off the native mussel populations.

DID YOU KNOW?

One-third of all Canadian residents depend on the Great Lakes for their water.

CIRCLE GAMES

And so it fell out, that very Night, the Crop of Oat shew'd as if it had all been of a flame: but next morning appear'd so neatly mow'd by the devil or some Infernal Spirit...

–Part of the inscription from "The Mowing Devil,"
a 1678 woodcutting Hertfordshire, England

Landing site of an unidentified flying object? Someone's idea of art? The result of vortex winds? Ball lightning strikes? A disturbance in the Earth's magnetic field? Seismic activity? A hoax to keep people occupied on a boring weekend? All of these have been put forward as explanations for the crop circles that began to demand public attention as early as the 1980s.

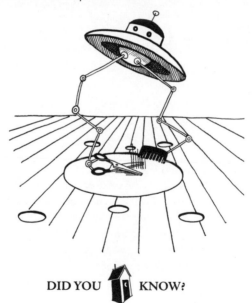

DID YOU KNOW?

Scientists have been unable to re-create, precisely, the vast majority of crop circle patterns that have been found to date.

Crazy 8s

The modern crop circle craze began in Britain when gigantic, flattened, figure-eight patterns in grain fields captured the attention of all but the most cynical and world-weary of Her Majesty's Loyal Citizens.

More and more...

The epidemic soon spread. But the phenomenon was not new to Canada. We had already been "visited." In Leeshore, AB, a small farming community about an hour's drive northeast of Edmonton, the first Canadian crop circle was reported in 1925. Since that time there have been nearly 250 reports from across Canada of mysterious designs in fields. And, curiouser and curiouser, the patterns, which have ranged in size from 3 metres to over 65 metres in length, are becoming more and more complex.

Not Circles At All

Many crop circles are not simple circles. Some are ovoid, slightly elongated, not-quite-round patterns; others are circles in combination with other circles or shapes. In 2004 alone, there were 18 confirmed reports of crop circles, and more than half of them were shapes other than simple circles. There were circles with outer rings, circles with radials, pictograms, half-circles adjacent to full circles, interlocking circles and in one case in Chilliwack, BC, a T-shape (90 metres long) with several small rectangles nearby.

Crop Circle Sightings (From East to West)

Nova Scotia—1	Northwest Territories—3
Prince Edward Island—2	Manitoba—26
New Brunswick—2	Saskatchewan—97
Québec—13	Alberta—34
Ontario—45	British Columbia—21

Other Weird Phenomena

Since 1925, crop circles have been seen in every province and territory except Newfoundland and Labrador, Yukon and Nunavut, although patterns listed as "Other Circular Phenomena" have been seen in all provinces between 1880 and 2005. These include circles and rings on frozen or semi-frozen lakes and creeks, and a large number of geometric shapes in fields where plants were burned to the roots, charred or simply vanished overnight.

So What's All the HOOPla?

It has been reported that birds will detour from their direct path to avoid flying over crop circles, and dogs often refuse to go into them. Dead flies are often found inside crop circles, and seed pods within the flattened areas are frequently empty, even though the plants themselves are bent but unharmed.

Quiz Question

What do you call someone who makes a study of crop circle phenomena?

A cereologist, the name derived from Ceres, the Roman goddess of agriculture.

And the seasons they go round and round
And the painted ponies go up and down
We're captive on the carousel of time
We can't return we can only look behind from where we came
And go round and round and round in the circle game.
–Joni Mitchell (1943–)
from "The Circle Game" sung by Buffy Sainte-Marie

JONI MITCHELL (Roberta Joan Anderson) was born November 7, 1943, in Fort Macleod, AB, and grew up in Saskatchewan. A leading figure in North American folk music throughout the 1970s and 1980s, Mitchell became the first Canadian woman named to the U.S. Rock & Roll Hall of Fame in 1997, was inducted into the Juno Hall of Fame in 1981 and received a Grammy Lifetime Achievement Award in 2002.

BUFFY SAINTE-MARIE was born February 20, 1941, on the Piapot Cree Reserve in Saskatchewan. Orphaned at a young age, she was adopted and raised in Maine and Massachusetts. A leading-edge singer and composer of protest sings in the 1960s and 1970s, she became a world-renowned folk hero and social activist. Over the years she has garnered numerous awards and recognitions: an honorary doctorate from the University of Regina, a medal from Queen Elizabeth II, a Juno and a Gemini. She earned an Oscar for her song "Up Where We Belong" and a National Aboriginal Lifetime Achievement Award in 1998.

With Mine Own Eyes—Some Intriguing Sightings

LANGENBURG, SK: 1974

Edwin Fuhr was working in his fields when he saw five large, metallic, dome-shaped objects hovering and swirling over his field. He got within 15 metres of them before they flew off, leaving five large flattened rings in the flax field.

CAMROSE, AB: 1967

Two girls reported seeing a cream-coloured object landing in a nearby pasture. A few weeks later, crop circles appeared in the same field. Investigators agreed that only a very heavy object from the air could have made the circles.

EAST GARAFAXA, ON: 2002

The sprouted grain inside the crop circles in Eugene Lammerding's barley field was analyzed by chromograph and found to hold an energy level 100 times that of the material outside the flattened areas.

Dancing Circles

Among the aboriginal groups of Canada, tribal dances frequently use the circle as a floor pattern symbolic of the circle of life, with the direction of the circle differing from one region to another. The Algonquians, for example, dance clockwise, while the Iroquois dance counterclockwise.

Hoop Dancing

A traditional form of dance among many aboriginal groups in Canada, the hoop dance is performed individually, in a thrilling representation of the circular and interdependent structure of the natural world. Dozens of hoops are added to the pattern the dancer holds aloft, each one representing the shape or movement of animals, birds, flowers and human beings in harmony with one another and with nature.

UNIDENTIFIED VISITORS

Signs of Intelligence?

A 1996 Angus Reid poll suggested that 70 percent of Canadians believe intelligent life exists elsewhere in the universe. More than 50 percent of Canadians say that Planet Earth has already had extraterrestrial visitors, and another 14 percent say unearthly aliens will visit in the next few years.

Eine Kleine Nacht-light

Kimberley, BC, known to skiers as Canada's Bavarian City, received some unwelcome visitors on the night of March 5, 1999. A diamond-shaped UFO with shimmering, flashing, coloured lights was seen by half a dozen witnesses just hours before the unexplained collapse, at midnight, of the roof of the abandoned McKim Theatre.

Welcome to St. Paul

Ladies and gentlemen, fasten your seat belts. We are approaching St. Paul, Alberta, and the world's first UFO landing pad. Please ensure that you don your human disguise before disembarking. We wouldn't want to frighten the locals.

Residents of St. Paul are making hay while the sun shines on their little community of 5000, located 200 kilometres northeast of Edmonton. The town's mascot is Zoot, a large, blue-eyed extraterrestrial, and local entrepreneurs have picked up on the ingenious marketing possibilities by giving their businesses names like Galaxy and Flying Saucer, building a Chamber of Commerce that looks like a space ship and hosting an international UFO conference.

Started as a centennial project, with construction of the UFO landing pad, the theme is bringing tourists by the tens of thousands to the area to see what exactly is going on—other than a few cattle and sheep mutilations, bumps in the night and the odd blood-curdling scream.

Put Your Trash into Orbit...10 minutes to Orbit...5 minutes to Orbit...

The Manitoba government had a clever anti-litter program, begun in the 1970s and abandoned some 20 years later, that cashed in on the UFO craze hitting the prairies. Situated along major highways, the orb-shaped garbage cans screamed out for people to use them, and use them they did. With the help of garbage bags made available at frequent spots along the road, travellers through Manitoba could gather up their garbage in the car and wait for the next "Orbit" site to be announced.

What Could They Be?

FORT MACLEOD, AB, AUGUST 27, 1956: While trying to set a new cross-country speed record in their F-86 Sabre jet, Royal Canadian Air Force pilot Robert Childerhose and his co-pilot Ralph Innes were flying in formation with three other planes at nearly 11,000 metres, at a speed of 740 km/hour, when Childerhose began taking photographs of some breathtaking thunderclouds gathering below them.

He noticed strange lights, and moments later, realized he was looking at a disc-shaped flying object that was glowing from its bottom side. Childerhose was able to take a photograph of the object before it disappeared from sight. When the plane landed, his sighting was confirmed by pilots in the other planes. The object in his photograph continues to defy experts, who have, to this day, been unable to positively identify it.

Sudbury and North Bay, ON, November 11, 1975:

In the early morning hours, police in Sudbury, ON, received numerous calls about three or four bright lights in the sky. People described the lights as huge, bright, cylindrical objects surrounded by smaller coloured lights, hovering at low altitudes. Other reports claimed the UFOs had chased them along roads in the area.

The most convincing report of all was received from the NORAD radar station at Canadian Forces Station Falconbridge in North Bay, where radar equipment tracked a number of unidentified flying objects. When several additional sightings were reported from American cities later the same day, the U.S. Air Force launched interceptor jets from Detroit, MI, to investigate. They found no evidence of any extraterrestrial objects other than the multiple eyewitness reports, but the sightings remain on file in both countries, with internal memos describing the sightings as "observed by reliable military personnel."

Shag Harbour, NS, October 4, 1967:

In the early evening, Nova Scotia's Barrington Passage RCMP detachment received a number of calls reporting a large craft flying very low and about to crash into the waters of Shag Harbour, southwest of Halifax. One of the first on the scene was Constable Ron Pond, who happened to be patrolling the area just before the crash and had seen the craft in the air, flying far faster than a plane, with an unusual array of lights and in an unfamiliar flight pattern.

When he arrived at the crash scene, he and the gathered crowd saw a large round object, glowing with a yellow light and floating in the bay about a kilometre from shore. By the time the Coast Guard and other boats reached the location, the object had sunk out of sight, leaving behind a distinct smell of sulphur in a ring of yellow foam. Divers from the RCMP and the Canadian Coast Guard were sent down to investigate, but no debris was ever found.

When the story hit the papers, another astonishing report was received. An Air Canada pilot, flying over southeastern Québec early on the evening of October 4, had seen a large object covered in brilliant lights. He reported hearing several explosions before losing sight of it.

LAND OF GIANTS AND MONSTERS

Sasquatch!

The Canadian version of the American "Bigfoot" or the Himalayan "Yeti," the Sasquatch is reported, by those who claim to have encountered it, to be a 2.5- to 3-metre-tall, upright, human-like animal covered in thick hair.

Many sightings have been accompanied by what witnesses report as "distinct vocalizations": loud, deep-toned, cough-like grunts or high-pitched shrieks. A peculiar and pungent odor is also sometimes reported.

Since the first documented reports in 1811, there have been hundreds of reported sightings. The jury is still out on the existence of the Sasquatch, since all of the video footage and footprints available for analysis have been inconclusive.

If You Knew Hairy...

The name "Sasquatch" is taken form the Coast Salish word *sas-kets*, meaning "hairy man," a prominent character in many of the tribal legends from the coastal regions of British Columbia. According to legend, a tribe of huge, very smelly, hairy men lurked in the valley forests, waiting for a chance to steal food.

Anthropologists have theorized that if such beings exist, they could be descendants of the giant ape *Gigantopithecus* that lived in southeast Asia more than 5 million years ago, long thought to be extinct. Most professionals are quick to dismiss the idea.

DOCUMENTED SASQUATCH SIGHTINGS IN CANADA

The Wendigo,
The Wendigo!
Its eyes are ice and indigo!
Its blood is rank and yellowish!
Its voice is hoarse and bellowish!

...

Last night it lurked in Canada;
Tonight, on your veranada!

–Ogden Nash (1902–71)

from "The Wendigo"

Although the Sasquatch is primarily a West Coast phenomenon, there are stories of another giant creature in the legends of various eastern First Nations. Depending on the linguistic group, it is referred to by some three dozen names, but all derive from the Algonquian word *witiku*, meaning both "evil spirit" and "cannibal."

The Windigo, a feared but revered elder brother figure, is a solitary, psychic, cannibalistic messenger that comes to warn people of impending doom or trials and to remind them of the evils of eating human flesh. It is generally described as 3 to 4 metres in height, with fang-like teeth and a lipless, misshapen mouth in an oversized head.

The Montagnais, in particular, have firm convictions concerning this evil manifestation and believe that it is a spirit-man, transformed after eating human flesh. Any contact with the Windigo will have one of two consequences: the human is either devoured or turned into a cannibal himself, with an insatiable appetite for human flesh.

Canada's Own Wolfman: The Loup-Garou

Stories of shape-changing humans had their beginnings with the arrival of French and other European settlers who brought the tales from home. Those people suspected of being werewolves, under a spell that caused them to transform into marauding wolves by night, were dealt with in much the same as witches—they were hunted down and killed, usually burned at the stake. Stories of loup-garou attacks were particularly prevalent in the valleys of the Laurentians. They typically told of hunters who failed to return from night expeditions or of children taken from their beds at night. Some old-timers who live in these regions still believe in the stories.

"Laisee-moi tranquille" Elmire she say "You mus' be crazy man."
"Yass—yass" I say "mebbe you t'ink I'm wan beeg loup garou,
Dat's forty t'ousand 'noder girl, I lef' dem all for you..."
–William Henry Drummond (1854–1907)
from "Le Vieux Temps"

William Henry Drummond was born in Ireland and came to Québec with his family at the age of 10. He became a medical doctor and in his spare time wrote lovingly and humorously about the Québec habitants, using a kind of "franglais" that entertained many but alienated some. In the spirit of political correctness, Drummond's work has been all but ignored in recent decades, but his light and lively poems, with their clever juxtaposition of French and English words, are a Canadian legacy. He was made a Fellow of the Royal Society of Canada in 1899. He received honorary degrees from the University of Toronto (1905) and Bishop's College (1905).

And Recent Studies Show...

In July 2005, a hair sample collected in the Yukon was sent to the University of Alberta for analysis. Thought at first to be a tuft of hair from a sasquatch, analysis proved that in fact the hair actually came from a North American bison. All Canada watched the news with anticipation for proof of the elusive "ape man's" existence, only to be disappointed yet again.

Quiz Question

What is cryptozoology?

The study of unknown animals.

Eh?...Two Brutes?

There is a legend of an enormous hairy creature called a Rugaru that lives in the swamps of Louisiana. Although the name sounds like the French word "loup-garou," the southern ogre is described as a bigfoot, while the northern one is a shape-changer.

> *I'm looking for the Ogopogo, the funny little Ogopogo,*
> *His mother was an earwig, his father was a whale;*
> *I'm going to put a little bit of salt upon his tail...*

The name for the Lake Okanagan creature was adopted in 1926 from an old British follies song called "I'm Looking for the Ogopogo."

There have been hundreds of sightings of the famed Ogopogo. Known for centuries as N'h-a-itk, the water god (pronounced *Nai-ta-ka* in English), by the local aboriginal Okanagans, Ogopogo continues to mystify even the most skeptical of observers with its sporadic appearances in Lake Okanagan.

Most sightings report a dark brown or black eel-like creature, approximately 10 to 15 metres long, with the ability to glide through the water quickly and effortlessly. Although some witnesses report humps on the creature's back, others say the humps are just the slim body of the animal undulating through the water.

All in the Family

Other Ogopogo family members seem to be turning up all over:
- Annepogo off Prince Edward Island
- Igopogo in Lake Simcoe, ON
- Manipogo in Manitoba's lake system
- Saskipogo in Lake Saskatchewan
- Sicopogo in Shuswap Lake, BC
- Tankopogo...don't turn around...

Quiz Question

What is dracontology?

The study of lake monsters.

No Kraken Jokes, eh!

Of all the sea-monster stories in Canada, few are as scientifically accepted as the tales of the Kraken, the giant squid from the Grand Banks of Newfoundland, first sighted in 1913. Reportedly close to 10 metres long and similar to the prehistoric *Architeuthis*, the Kraken is mentioned in E.J. Pratt's 1926 narrative poem "The Cachalot," in which Pratt describes a violent battle, which he claimed to have witnessed, between a sperm whale (in French: *cachalot*) and a giant squid.

E.J. (Edwin John) Pratt (1882–1964) was born in Western Bay, NL, and educated at Victoria College and the University of Toronto. His first published work, *Newfoundland Verses* (1923), and more than a dozen later volumes of poetry established him as one of the dominant Canadian poets of the 20th century.

The Creature of Lake Memphremagog

Affectionately known as Memphré, the sea serpent is described by witnesses as a 7- to 20-metre-long, three-humped, black or dark brown creature resembling a plesiosaurus, which once roamed the prehistoric Laurentian Shield. Settlers in Vermont and Québec were the first Europeans to report sightings in the 1840s, but the beast had been part of the legends of local native groups for centuries.

Lake Memphremagog, a deep, cold lake straddling the Canada-United States border south of Magog, QC, has been the site of numerous encounters. By 1995 there were 215 documented sightings of the creature, and the sightings continue. In 1996 alone, Memphré was seen on 10 occasions and by dozens of people. The creature did not seem at all shy about the attention, as it created turbulence in full view of startled spectators.

Hardly Utopian

As far back as the 1800s there have been sightings of a snapping sea creature in Lake Utopia, NB. Apparently fond of the cold, this creature, as yet unnamed, makes its appearance soon after the ice breaks up in the spring, occasionally breaching the melting ice with its enormous tooth-filled mouth, in search of fresh food.

Monsters Worth 39 Cents

Canada Post's 1990 stamp series features a collection of Canadian monsters including Ogopogo, the Sasquatch and the Loup-Garou.

Some Big Fish Story

There have been numerous reported sightings since the 1960s of a fairly large (3 to 10 metres long), unusual animal in Turtle Lake, SK. Some witnesses say its head resembles that of a sea horse; others, that of a seal. It has been described as black, brown or green. Whatever it looks like, it is big and has been blamed for everything from destroying fishing nets to attempting to capsize boats.

CELEBRATIONS

Powwow

Traditional ceremonial gatherings, powwows are celebrated in one form or another by all First Nations groups in Canada. Although changed somewhat over the decades in order to welcome Canadian tourists as well as visitors from other countries, they still maintain most of the traditional features from centuries ago, and all retain a very important spiritual component, much of which is demonstrated in dance.

Powwow dancing is not just an activity performed for entertainment; it is a way of life. In their training by elders, powwow dancers learn far more than just dance steps. They are educated in customs and in spiritual understandings based on traditional teachings that will permit them to lead good lives and become strong leaders.

DID YOU  KNOW?

Many costumes worn by dancers at a powwow are adorned with feathers, which are highly respected items among First Nations people. If a feather is dropped during any part of a performance, the performance is halted until a special ceremony is performed, usually by an elder dancer accompanied by drum song, in which the feather is respectfully retrieved.

Mummering

A Newfoundland custom with roots among the first Irish and English settlers in the province, mummering is traditionally practised around Christmas. Their identities hidden by masks or hooded cast-off garments, and sometimes dressed up as the opposite sex, both men and women go from house to house, playing fiddles and other musical instruments, and singing and dancing to entertain the occupants. Mummers always get a snack and a glass of wine, usually homemade, before moving on to the next house. Part of the fun for the hosts is guessing the identities of the guests, who, once identified, have to remain unmasked for the remainder of the visit.

Money Walks...Down the Aisle

Of the 1.1 million single adults in Canada between 28 and 55 years of age, 50 percent do not expect to marry. Those who do not expect to marry tend to have lower annual incomes ($29,700 compared to $34,400) and less education (24 percent compared to 34 percent with university degrees) than those who expect to walk down the aisle.

DID YOU  KNOW?

In Wawa, ON, it is against the law to show affection in public on Sunday!

Day of Rest... and No Romance Please!

In Canada, nearly 60 percent of all weddings are held in summer. Twenty percent take place in August. Sunday was the traditional wedding day until the early 17th century, when religious groups protested that it was wrong to have celebrations of any kind on the Lord's Day. Now, close to 75 percent of the weddings in Canada take place on Saturday.

Honeymoon

It was accepted practice in Babylon, 4000 years ago, that for a month after the wedding, the bride's father would supply his son-in-law with all the honey mead he could drink. Since the calendar was based on the phases of the moon, this period was called the honey month, now known as the honeymoon.

Today, Canadians tend to celebrate the post-wedding period very differently from ancient peoples. Close to 96 percent of all modern couples choose to travel in conjunction with their big day. Trips are either taken immediately after their wedding, or, as is the case for more and more Canadian couples, the exchange of vows takes place in an exotic location in a new trend referred to by the travel industry as the Destination Wedding.

Potlatch

A tradition practised by all Northwest Coast First Nations, the potlatch was an extremely important gathering held to celebrate inauguration of tribal leaders or initiation of warriors or to mourn a death. Potlatches were also used as trade opportunities within and between groups. They featured dancing, dramatic and humorous skits, and feasting. Potlatches were banned by the Canadian government in 1884 and were not sanctioned again until 1951.

Potluck

Purported to be a modern-day reincarnation of the potlatch, the Canadian potluck supper is a loosely planned event where each guest brings a dish of his or her own choosing. The modern potluck supper bears little resemblance to the grand and significant aboriginal potlatches, which were often planned years in advance. Many lasted several days, solidifying trade and cultural ties among groups who might not see one another for months at a time.

Spooky Spending

Hallowe'en is the second biggest holiday of the year in Canada (after Christmas) in terms of retail sales. With 85 percent of the population participating, we spend over $800 million each year on Hallowe'en: $200 million of it for sweets to give out at the door and the remainder on costumes, decorations and cards.

STAMPEDE!

"The Greatest Outdoor Show on Earth"

It all started when a trick roper named Guy Weadick galloped into Calgary one summer's day in 1912 and convinced local cattle barons to let him use their Calgary exhibition grounds for his week-long "Greatest Outdoor Show on Earth." With the addition, in 1923, of the popular chuckwagon races, Weadick presented cowgirls and cowboys, trick ropers, bronc riders and costumed Natives in a Wild West show that since became famous all over the world.

No Longer "Just a Rodeo"

Today, the 10-day Stampede, complete with high-level entertainment headlined by major country and western stars, has become one of the main draws for summer travel in the west. With an annual average of 1.25 million spectators in attendance, it now offers more than $1 million in competition prize money.

Known as "Montana Slim" in the United States, Nova Scotian Wilf Carter (1904–96) was a lumberjack, guitar player and yodelling singer-songwriter. Regarded as the father of Canadian country music, he got his start on radio in Stampede City in 1930 and performed and recorded regularly across Canada and the United States, giving his last tour, "The Last Round-Up Tour," in 1991 at the age of 86.

Blue Rodeo, the Canadian country rock band with a unique and ever-evolving sound, has sold close to 4 million records since its beginnings in the 1970s.

Not Just Clowning Around

Clowns are essential for rodeo safety. They not only entertain the crowds and occasionally move required equipment into position, but they also protect thrown riders by leading riderless animals out of the ring.

In bull-riding events, clowns specially trained in bullfighting are used to distract the bull when the rider dismounts or is thrown.

Canadian Royalty

Blackie and the Rodeo Kings, a roots-rock trio named in honour of a piece by Canadian singer-songwriter Willie P. Bennett, were awarded a Juno in 2000 for their CD "Kings of Love." They continue to record and tour, playing their own original material, as well as compositions by other Canadian songwriters including Fred Eaglesmith, Bruce Cockburn and Murray McLauchlan.

Pro Rodeo Event Lexicon

Saddle bronc riding

The rider is required to stay on board a feisty bucking bronco until the bronc gives up or the crowd goes home.

Bareback riding

Same as above, but without the benefit of a nice padded saddle. Ouch!

Bull riding

Same as above, only the rider is atop a very large, very agitated, intact male member of the cattle family. (No saddle.)

Tie-down roping

The calf runs, the horse follows, the rider ropes and jumps and, if all goes well, ties up three of the calf's legs before it can get away.

Steer wrestling

Same as above, sort of. Steer runs, horse follows, rider jumps, steer runs over cowboy. Steer wins.

Barrel racing

The only ladies-only event in pro rodeo. Female rider on horseback runs a cloverleaf pattern around three barrels and makes it back to the bunkhouse in time to cook dinner.

Team roping

Two cowboys and two horses work together to trick a running steer into letting himself be hog-tied.

FRUITS 🍇 BERRIES

There's a thing we love to think of
when the summer days are long,
And the summer winds are blowing,
and the summer sun is strong,
When the orchards and the meadows
throw their fragrance on the air,
When the grain-fields flaunt their riches,
and the glow is everywhere.

–Jean Blewett (1872-1934) from "There's a Thing We Love"

Jean (McKishnie) Blewett, Canadian poet, was born at Scotia, Lake Erie, Ontario, on November 4, 1872. Her writing, mostly poetry on simple subjects such as the land, harvest and nature, became popular while she was still in her teens. A number of her works, such as "There's a Thing We Love," were published in school readers during the early part of the 20th century.

An Apple a Day...but not just any old apple

Red Delicious apples are the most nutritious apple variety grown in Ontario. Both the skin and flesh are highly nutritious and contain twice the antioxidants of the Empire, the apple with the lowest level of antioxidants in a recent study of the eight main Ontario-grown varieties.

RANKING IN ANTIOXIDANT ACTIVITY
From highest to lowest

Apple Skin	Apple Flesh
Red Delicious	Northern Spy
Ida Red	Cortland
Cortland	Red Delicious
Northern Spy	McIntosh
Golden Delicious	Ida Red
Mutsu	Golden Delicious
McIntosh	Mutsu
Empire	Empire

DID YOU  KNOW?

The Delicious variety ranks second only to the McIntosh in popularity for the Canadian consumer.

Canada's Big Apple — a real Big Mac!
McIntosh apples, affectionately known as Macs, make up close to half of this country's annual apple crop. They are the only variety grown in every one of the five apple-growing districts in Canada.

The McIntosh Story — a Romantic Canadian Tale

In 1811, young John McIntosh, a Scottish-born settler in Dundela in eastern Ontario, was clearing his land when he discovered a patch of what he recognized as apple-tree seedlings. He transplanted them into his garden and waited for spring snows to melt. Sadly, only one small tree survived the winter, but he nursed it, and within a few years it produced a unique apple, crisp and sweet-tart with deep red skin.

John's sons Allen and Sandy learned grafting techniques and began grafting branches from their father's wonderful apple tree into crabapple seedlings, which were sowed the following spring. By 1845, the two younger McIntosh men had taken over the farm and were producing and selling their popular stock, which became known as McIntosh Reds.

Today there are more than three million McIntosh apple trees in North America. All of them are directly descended from that one little tree that John McIntosh found on his plot of land. Despite being singed in an 1895 fire that ran through the McIntosh orchard, that original tree survived and continued to produce fruit until 1906. A small stone marker still stands on the old McIntosh farm, nearly hidden by weeds. It reads:"The site of the original McIntosh apple tree 1811–1906."

 Apples are Canada's largest fruit crop, with an estimated 400,000 tonnes grown every year.

Canadian Domestic Apple Production
by Volume
(in thousands of metric tonnes (mt): 1 mt = 1000 kg)

	1995	1996	1997	1998	1999	2000	2001	2002	2003	2004*
British Columbia	159.2	151.6	121.7	178.5	132.7	131.2	129.7	126.6	131.5	128.4
Ontario	294.4	193.4	246.3	229.0	331.3	262.9	241.5	177.0	145.2	140.6
Québec	96.1	85.5	86.0	70.9	119.0	89.6	71.5	63.9	98.3	87.1
New Brunswick	5.2	4.4	4.0	3.6	4.8	5.1	4.0	5.0	4.6	5.0
Nova Scotia	53.3	48.3	45.0	42.3	46.0	41.7	35.4	39.3	36.3	33.4
Canada	608.2	483.3	503.6	524.7	634.3	531.1	482.5	412.2	416.2	395.0

* Preliminary figures

Canada's Five Main Apple-Growing areas
- ☞ Annapolis Valley, Nova Scotia
- ☞ Saint John River Valley, New Brunswick
- ☞ Southern Québec
- ☞ St. Lawrence Valley to the lower Great Lakes of southern Ontario
- ☞ Okanagan Valley, British Columbia

DID YOU KNOW?

In Newfoundland folklore, it is recommended that dead dogs be buried under fruit trees to ensure a good harvest.

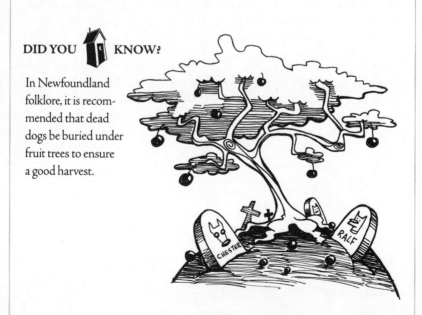

CANADA'S BREAD BASKET

Dost thou think because thou art virtuous,
there shall be no more cakes?

–William Shakespeare, *Twelfth Night*

The above quote appeared, along with many others from various sources, in the 1905 edition of *Ogilvie's Book for a Cook,* the first widely distributed Canadian cookbook. Canadians were reminded throughout the little book that by using Ogilvie Royal Household Flour, they were feeding their family with the same product the Ogilvie company supplied, by Royal Warrant, to HRH The Prince of Wales (later King George V).

The Ogilvie Flour Mills Company began in 1855, when Alexander and John Ogilvie took over management of their father's milling company, which had its start in Jacques Cartier, QC. A third son, William Watson Ogilvie, joined them in 1860, and they managed to compete with large Minneapolis millers to provide flour for Britain from their mills in Ontario, Montréal and Winnipeg. In the 1870s, the introduction of a special grade of hard red spring wheat established Ogilvie's reputation as provider of the world's best pastry and bread flour. By 1895, Ogilvie was the largest privately owned flour-milling company in the world.

Canadian Grain and Oilseed Production (in kilotonnes*), 2003–04

Wheat	23,552
Barley	12,328
Corn	9587
Canola	6669
Oats	3691
Soybeans	2268
Flaxseed	754
Rye	327

* Thousand tonnes

Wheat is, by far, Canada's most important economic crop, grown commercially in every province except Newfoundland and Labrador. Canada exports wheat around the globe and ties with Australia and the European Union for second place in the world, after the United States, in quantity of wheat exported.

Real Heroes

The average two-slice sandwich today contains 15 percent more bread than it did 20 years ago. Although loaf sizes remain much the same, manufacturers have been gradually increasing the thickness of each slice.

Our Daily Bread

Despite a decline in its consumption in recent years (65.5 kg/person in 2003 compared to 69.7 kg/person in 2002, constituting a 6 percent decline), bread continues to be the most widely consumed grain product in Canada.

Fading Prairie Silhouettes

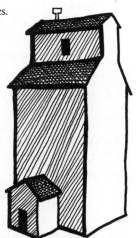

The wooden grain elevator was once the symbol of the prairies. Standing tall and majestic in a field of golden grain, the grain elevator signalled to the world the prairie farmer's reliance on the land. Dotting the landscape in an array of bright colours along the country's railway lines and usually emblazoned with the town's name, there were nearly 6000 elevators on the Canadian prairies by the mid 1930s.

With changes in technology and demand, most wooden elevators have either been replaced by concrete structures or abandoned entirely. There are fewer than 100 wooden grain elevators operating in Canada today.

How Does a Grain Elevator Work?

Traditional wooden elevators typically consist of a tall, gable-roofed structure that is often attached to one or more smaller annexes, or outbuildings, with various uses: office space, scales or equipment and fuel storage.

The main structure houses a series of separate, upright storage bins and one large-capacity basin known as "the pit." Grain is weighed, then dumped from the farmer's truck into the pit. From there, it is transported up "the leg"—an endless series of buckets attached to a mechanical elevating belt—and deposited by the "gerber," a funnel-shaped distributor, into an empty bin or one holding similar grain. To ship the grain, the procedure is reversed.

In the 1930s, Saskatchewan Wheat Pool, a farmer-owned elevator company, was the largest producer cooperative in the world.

GOLD RUSH

There are strange things done in the midnight sun
By the men who moil for gold;
The Arctic trails have their secret tales
That would make your blood run cold...

–Robert W. Service (1874–1958)

from "The Cremation of Sam McGee"

Robert William Service immigrated to Canada from Scotland in 1894. An experienced bank worker, he was able to find a job in 1903 with the Canadian Bank of Commerce (now CIBC). He was transferred to Dawson, YT, where gold rush fever inspired his poems, first published in 1907 as *Songs of a Sourdough*. Poems such as "The Cremation of Sam McGee" and "The Shooting of Dan McGrew" earned him the nickname "Poet of the Yukon."

Cheque This Out!

A personal cheque for $7.75, dated April 23, 1912, and signed by Robert W. Service, was appraised at $300 to $450 CDN in early 2005. Not considered a rare, informative document, it is still of interest to collectors of Service and gold rush memorabilia.

There's Gold in Them Thar Hills

The gold rushes of 19th-century Canada were largely responsible for the creation of two of Canada's largest territories—British Columbia and Yukon. In 1857, gold was found on the Fraser River, and the great influx of Americans seeking their fortune caused the British government to react by creating the colony of British Columbia in 1858, giving Britain control over laws and regulations concerning claims.

Several small rushes followed until the Fraser River gold finds began to dwindle. In 1860, gold was found near Cariboo Lake. The subsequent building of the trail known as the Cariboo Road gave access for people from different areas of Canada to moil for gold.

In 1896, gold was found along Rabbit Creek (later named Bonanza Creek) by members of the local Tagish tribe, Tagish Charley, Skookum Jim, Jim's sister Shaaw Tláa (Kate) and Kate's husband, George Carmack. The great influx of gold prospectors became known as the Klondike Gold Rush, the last major gold rush. The massive population explosion in the Yukon—from 5000 people to over 30,000—that resulted from the gold rush led to the establishment of the Yukon Territory in 1898.

Barkerville's Beginnings

In 1862, William "Billy" Barker, a sailor from Cornwall, England, made a huge gold strike on the Fraser River in BC's Cariboo region. Although most of the claims had been staked by the time he arrived, he persisted, striking a seam that paid out what would be equivalent to over $7 million today. Barker's find enticed more gold hunters, and by 1865, the town that was named in his honour had a population of 3000, with its own movie theatres, banks, a Hudson's Bay store and a Masonic Lodge. The town is now a provincial historic park.

NOTE! This gold-mining Billy Barker is not to be confused with William George "Billy" Barker (1894–1930), World War I flying ace born in Dauphin, MB, who was credited with 53 aerial victories, including a single-handed air battle against some 60 German aircraft, a feat that earned him the Victoria Cross at the age of 24.

DID YOU  KNOW?

The Klondike Gold Rush lasted only 18 months.

A three-kilometre stretch of one tributary alone, Eldorado Creek, produced over $30 million worth of gold during the height of the Klondike rush. It is known as the richest gold creek find in the world.

Klondike Kate (1869–1932)

Katherine Ryan was born August 29, 1869, in Johnville, NB. After training as a nurse, she spent several months nursing in a hospital in Washington state, where she developed a bad case of gold fever. After outfitting herself in Vancouver, she travelled to the Yukon gold fields in search of fortune. She staked a number of claims within the first few months of her arrival and left her mark on the mostly male Klondike population.

Not only was Katherine the first female member of the North-West Mounted Police and, at one time, the Klondike's jail keeper, she was also the first female gold inspector for the Yukon and a part-time camp doctor, performing surgeries on prospectors who were wounded in the line of battle for gold. She died in Vancouver at the age of 63.

No Diets Please

Cecile Marion, a Klondike dancehall girl who knew her net worth, agreed to marry gold miner Chris Johansen in exchange for her weight in gold. Her price came to $25,000. He happily paid up.

Some Triumphed, Some Failed

☞ A second woman laid claim to the moniker "Klondike Kate." Kate Rockwell, a dancehall girl, also took the nickname for herself after she was arrested for prostitution and, while in jail, met Kate Ryan, in her role as a "constable special" for the NWMP.

☞ On April 13, 1898, at the height of the Klondike Gold Rush, an avalanche in the Chilkoot Pass killed 60 gold-seekers travelling from their claims to the cities to purchase supplies or trade their gold for cash.

☞ Belinda Mulrooney, an Irish-born American whose dog was the inspiration for American novelist Jack London's animal character in *Call of the Wild*, travelled to the Klondike in 1897 with luxury goods she sold for $30,000, enough to set up a restaurant to feed the masses. On opening day she made $6000. She later purchased a hotel and a rich gold claim, and within a short time, she became one of Dawson's wealthiest citizens. She returned to the United States with her fortune, but it eventually ran out. She died alone and in poverty in Seattle at the age of 95.

☞ A party of 19 wealth-seekers from New York state set out in late 1896 from Alaska, across the mammoth St. Elias Mountains, towards the Klondike. During the voyage, 15 members of the group either vanished into crevices in the ice, died in avalanches, went insane from fear or died of fever and scurvy. Only four men survived the trek, all of whom were left totally or partially blind from snow blindness. None of the group made it to the Klondike.

PIRATES & PILFERED PENCE

From Peter the Pirate to Peter the Peer

Harbour Grace, NF, the quiet, picturesque, seaside village just northwest of present-day St. John's, was home to one of the most notorious pirates ever to sail the seas. Peter Easton, a British-born aristocrat and officer, turned to piracy in the early 1600s when peace with Spain resulted in the withdrawal of the royal privateering charter that had given him licence to plunder in the name of the Crown.

Gathering together hundreds of unemployed men who had been involved in legal raiding and plundering for the British Crown during the war, Easton ran one of the most successful pirate confederacies of the time, looting ships with amazing courage and frightening accuracy from his headquarters in Newfoundland. By 1610 he commanded some 1400 men and 10 well-equipped warships.

In 1618, Easton gave up pirateering and moved to Ville Franche, France, where he married a French noblewoman and adopted the title Marquis of Savoie. It is estimated that his fortune was worth close to $600 million CDN at the time of his death.

The Treasure of Black Hole Harbour

A treasure was supposedly buried by Norwegian pirates more than 200 years ago in a slit cave carved into the side of Haunted Falls near Baxter Harbour, NS. Inaccessible because of its location below sea level for all but a few days a year, the cave apparently holds stones engraved with mysterious markings that no one has been able to decipher.

The Ghost Ship *Malignant*

When the light is right and the spirit is willing, the ghost of the pirate ship *Malignant* can be seen off the Nova Scotia coast from a small village some 19 kilometres south of Antigonish, in a cove that now bears the name of the unfortunate ship that sank there in the 17th century. Some believe the ghostly vision, with its burning sails, is a reminder of the poor sailors who lost their lives when their pirate captain ordered them to scuttle *Malignant* rather than hand over the riches on board to the pursuing British warship. Mi'kmaq elders claim the sighing of the sea in that area is the sound of sprits sent to guard the treasure from the many looters who have visited the site over the decades.

The Treasure Pit of Oak Island

Since 1795 there have been thousands of attempts to find the elusive treasure supposedly buried in a pit on Oak Island, an uninhabited, 60-hectare island just off the eastern coast of Nova Scotia in Mahone Bay. No one seems clear on how the rumour of treasure began, but the fact that the pit is guarded by a series of clever handmade booby traps is a sure sign that something important is hidden there. The traps consist of a series of interconnected channels that cause the pit to fill with sea water whenever anyone tries to dig in it.

Searchers during the 19th century uncovered enough material to make continued searching an enticing prospect: there were log platforms at various depths beneath the ground and layer after layer of packing material, which included coconut husks. Later investigation uncovered a cement vault and an iron barrier that sit at a depth of over 50 metres, but they were inundated with sea water within minutes of being uncovered.

Among the famous people lured to Oak Island's treasure were Hollywood screen pirate Errol Flynn, former U.S. president Franklin D. Roosevelt as well as quick-drawing hero John Wayne.

Six people have died since the 1800s in their attempts to find the treasure. But beware. Legend suggests that the pit will not give up its prize until the seventh victim dies.

DID YOU KNOW?

Martin Frobisher came to Canada in the 16th century in search of the Northwest Passage. The famed explorer discovered Resolution Island, claimed Baffin Island for the British and was the man for whom Frobisher Bay was named. He was also a pirate—one of the sailors paid by the British government to loot and pillage in the name of the Crown.

Kidd's Koffers

Many say the booty of the notorious pirate Captain William Kidd, who plied the east coast of North America from Newfoundland to Florida during the late 1600s, lies buried somewhere on Pomquet Island, off Nova Scotia's coast. It is believed that Kidd found the isolated spot and buried his pirated treasure where only he would find it. According to local legend, Captain Kidd's spirit guards the hidden chests.

LIQUOR

Signs of the Times

Until the late 1960s in Canada, women who were unaccompanied by a male companion were not permitted to enter drinking establishments. Most bars had two distinct entrances: one marked "Men" and one for "Ladies & Escorts."

Alcohol

Also known as hooch, spirits, booze, firewater, nip, tipple or simply drink, alcoholic beverages are enjoyed by a fair number of Canadians. Nearly 2.7 billion litres of alcoholic beverages were sold at outlets across Canada in 2001–02.

For some, alcohol abuse is a problem. It is estimated that approximately 641,000 people in Canada display symptoms of alcohol dependency, and every year, people who have consumed too much alcohol are responsible for deaths, injuries and destruction of property.

Legal Age Notwithstanding...

In 2002, an estimated 641,000 Canadians, or about 2.6 percent of the population aged 15 or older, reported symptoms suggesting that they were dependent on alcohol.

DID YOU  **KNOW?**

Hooch comes from the name of a small, Northwest Coast Tlingit tribe, the *Hutsnuwu* (pronounced *Hoo-chee-noo* by English speakers). The word originally referred to the particularly powerful potable beverage the Hutsnuwu brewed from molasses. The word later came into general use as a term for alcohol.

Percentage of Canadians Who Likely Meet the Criteria for Alcohol Dependence

	TOTAL	MEN	WOMEN
Canada	2.6	3.8	1.3
British Columbia	3.6	5.0	2.2
Alberta	3.5	4.9	2.1
Saskatchewan	4.1	6.0	2.2
Manitoba	3.6	5.3	1.9
Ontario	2.1	3.3	1.0
Québec	1.9	2.9	1.0
New Brunswick	2.0	3.2	0.9
Nova Scotia	3.2	5.5	1.0
Prince Edward Island	2.8	4.1	1.5
Newfoundland/Labrador	3.2	5.5	1.0

(Based on a 2002 community health survey by Statistics Canada. The Yukon, Northwest Territories and Nunavut were not included in the survey.)

This Is the Law!

In Canada it is illegal for advertisers to promote consumption of alcohol, to suggest that it will enhance enjoyment of any activity or to imply that it will promote social or business success.

Insinuations of Higher Learning

While 11 percent of Canadians with less than high school education consume 14+ drinks per week, only 7 percent of university graduates consume the same quantity.

However...

While 68 percent of Canadians in the highest income group drink regularly, and only 9 percent are abstainers, only 40 percent of those in the lowest income group drink regularly, and 18 percent abstain.

When and Where Are You Legal?

PROVINCE	LEGAL DRINKING AGE	WAS	WHEN CHANGED
Newfoundland/Labrador	19	21	July 1972
Prince Edward Island	19	18	July 1987
Nova Scotia	19	21	April 1971
New Brunswick	19	21	August 1972
Québec	18	20	July 1972
Ontario	19	18	January 1979
Manitoba	18	21	August 1970
Saskatchewan	19	18	September 1976
Alberta	18	21	April 1971
British Columbia	19	21	April 1970
Northwest Territories	19	21	July 1970
Yukon	19	21	February 1970
Nunavut	19	n/a	

Screeching-In

A favourite tradition in Newfoundland, the screeching-in ceremony involves kissing a codfish and then downing a drink of strong Newfoundland screech (doubtless to wash away the memory of cold, dead, fish lips). Once the fish is properly smooched, the inductee to the Royal Society of Screechers is then required to repeat a bit of tongue-twisting foolishness before being slapped on the back, welcomed to the island as an honorary Newfoundlander and presented with a frameable certificate to take back home to the envy of all.

And Just What Is Screech?

Apparently named for the ear-splitting howl of an exuberant imbiber from centuries past, Newfoundland screech is strong, dark, Jamaica-style rum.

Hail Caesar!

A Calgary bartender, Walter Chell, created the Caesar cocktail in 1969 using vodka and Clamato juice. More than 250 million Caesars are sold every year in Canada, making it our country's best-selling cocktail.

LOTS OF SUDS
THIS PAGE IS DEDICATED TO ALL DIEHARD
TEGESTOLOGISTS*

It's Just Suds—But We Win!

Both regular Canadian (5.0 percent alcohol) and light Canadian beer (4.5 percent alcohol) are stronger than American regular and light beers, which come in at a level of 4.5 percent and 4.0 percent alcohol-by-volume respectively.

Canada's Brewing History

Beer was first introduced to Canada by European settlers in the 17th century. The first commercial brewery was built in Québec City by Jean Talon in 1668, followed by other breweries across eastern Canada:

John Molson .... Montréal 1786

Alexander Keith .... Halifax 1829

Thomas Carling .... London, ON 1840

John Labatt .... London, ON 1847

Eugene O'Keefe .... Toronto........... 1862

Quiz Question

What is a tegestologist?

A tegestologist is a beer coaster collector.

Hopping Lightly

Maybe it was Twiggy, that pencil-thin model from the '60s, who started it all, but in the early '70s, fashion attention began to stray upward from hemlines to waist-lines, and the decades of the weight-watchers began. In a move that brought guf-faws from veteran beer drinkers across the nation, the Labatt Brewing Company, in 1973, introduced Canada's first light beer. It was a hard sell.

The early ad campaigns for Cool Lite tried for a bit of "light" humour with a skepti-cal pitch that may have reflected the company's own misgivings:

"Who's going to drink it? Maybe it's for you."

By 1977, sales were promising, and Labatt changed the name of its light product to Special Lite, with a new pitch line: "It's here!"

The Great Canadian Suds Debate

Light beer caught on in a big way south of the border. But Canadian beer drinkers were slower to buy into it, and the battle in the marketplace was only one of the battles Labatt had to wage. The Canada Food and Drugs Act declared that to be considered "light," beer had to be low in calories and contain no more than 2.5 percent alcohol. Even though it was lower in calories, Labatt Special Lite was more then 4.0 percent alcohol.

In 1979, Labatt challenged the federal government's definition of "light" beer as unconstitutional, and battle was waged in the Supreme Court. In December of that year, the Supreme Court of Canada ruled 6 to 3 in favour of Labatt and found that the Food and Drugs Act's regulations concerning the brewing of beer were invalid.

Here's the Skinny On It!

Today, most major brewing companies in Canada produce light beers, which, on average, contain one-third fewer calories than most regular beers (100 vs 150).

DID YOU KNOW?

Roughly 20 percent of beer consumed by Canadians is light, whereas light beer constitutes over 50 percent of the beer consumed by Americans.

A Case for Beer

Drink up. It's good for you! Beer contains amino acids, vitamins, proteins, carbohy-drates and minerals. Studies have shown that light to moderate beer-drinking (one to two glasses a day) can have beneficial effects on health, possibly reducing the likelihood of developing coronary heart disease and coronary artery disease.

Close But No Cigar!

Prohibition laws affected beer as well as liquor. Near-beer, a malt beverage containing less than 0.5 percent alcohol, was first served legally in Canada in 1919 because it was weak enough to be considered non-alcoholic. When spruced up with alcohol, it was called "spiked beer," and although it was illegal, spiked beer became quite popular until 1925, when the sale of beer by the glass was again legalized.

DID YOU  KNOW?

Consumed by more than 10 million Canadians a year, beer is Canada's fourth most popular beverage after water, milk and coffee.

Strange Brew!

The "Great White North" segment, featuring Second City TV's fictional beer-guzzling characters Bob and Doug McKenzie, was the genesis of their 1983 movie *Strange Brew*.

A Heap of Suds

During the 18th century, British soldiers in Canada were given a ration of six pints of beer a day to keep up their strength and, presumably, their spirits.

Now That's Big Beer Bucks!

More beer is sold in Canada than all other alcoholic beverages combined! Of some $14.5 billion spent in Canada on alcoholic beverages in the 2001–02 fiscal year, over 51 percent was spent on beer.

Canadian, eh?
...being a brief lesson in Canadian drinking terminology

☞ Twofer: A case of 24 beers (also pronounced "two-four" by those who have had elocution lessons)

☞ May 2-4: The Victoria Day holiday, formerly celebrated on May 24, but now on the second-last weekend in May; the 2-4 designation not only suggests the old date, but is also a reference to the tradition of consumption, over the holiday weekend, of multiple cases of 24 beers

☞ 26er (also known as two-six): A 750 ml (26 oz) bottle of alcohol

☞ 40 (also known as a 40-pounder): A 1.14 L (40 oz) bottle of alcohol

☞ 66er (aka "gripper" because of the indented side handles): A 1.89 L (66 oz) bottle of alcohol

Beer Consumption by Province for 2001–02 (litres/person)

Yukon	144.2
Newfoundland/Labrador	95.2
Québec	94.0
Alberta	90.0
Northwest Territories and Nunavut	84.3
Prince Edward Island	82.6
Ontario	81.9
New Brunswick	81.3
Nova Scotia	79.0
Manitoba	77.9
Saskatchewan	76.8
British Columbia	75.9

Canada ranks 20th in the world in its annual consumption of beer. (The top five beer-consuming nations, in order of volume, are the Czech Republic, Germany, Denmark, Austria, Ireland.)

DID YOU KNOW?

The first patent processed in Canada by the Canadian government was issued to G. Riley on July 6, 1842. The patent was for an improved method of brewing beer and malt liquors.

Two Stomachs, Anyone?

Cows have extremely complex stomachs that break down the alcohol in beer, turning it into non-alcoholic food energy. A cow can consume many litres of beer without any resulting increase in blood-alcohol levels.

Short Neck, Short Life

Shorter, and with a larger diameter than the long-necked bottle, short-necked beer bottles called "stubbies" came into use in Canada in 1962. It was argued that although the stubby held the same volume, its shape made it harder to break and easier to store and handle. Nevertheless, between 1982 and 1984, most beer companies moved back to the conventional long-necked type.

PROHIBITION!

Everything that was wrong then is all legal now.
It makes you, over a long life time,
wonder who the heck was right and who wasn't.
–Moon Mullin (1910–2003)

Laurence "Moon" Mullin, a Moose Jaw, SK, resident, was said to have been a "tunnel crawler," one of the kids recruited (and paid well) to deliver messages, transport liquor and run errands for bootleggers and gamblers who lived under the town in the tunnels during Prohibition. Among his "employers" were Diamond Jim Brady and members of Al Capone's gang.

There were rumours that Al Capone himself frequented the Moose Jaw tunnels, but no proof of his presence there was ever found. In fact, when questioned on the subject, Capone answered: "I don't even know what street Canada is on."

"Demon Rum" and Prohibition

In the days before adequate social welfare systems, the effects of alcohol abuse on families and individuals were even worse than they are today. In 1878, under pressure from various anti-drinking groups, including the Women's Christian Temperance Union, the Canadian government instituted the Scott Act (Canada Temperance Act). The act allowed any municipality to prohibit, by majority vote, the sale of liquor.

By the turn of the century, so many municipalities had made liquor illegal that all provinces closed drinking establishments and prohibited, to some extent, the sale and consumption of alcohol. Liquor continued to be produced in Canada, but its sale was strictly controlled by government. Alcohol could be acquired for medicinal use, but a doctor's prescription was required.

Blind Pigs and Moonshine Stills

In response to the limited availability of liquor, home brewing became popular. Illicit beverage rooms, known as speakeasies or blind pigs (see page 91 for definition), served both home brew and illegally acquired good-quality liquor.

Rum-running

By 1919, most Canadians had had enough of the liquor limitations imposed by the government, and over the next 10 years, Prohibition died a slow death, province-by-province. During those years, Canada's rejection of Prohibition became a problem for the United States, which had gone nationwide and strict in its fight against drinking. Although it was against the law for anyone to transport, sell or produce liquor anywhere in the United States, it was no longer illegal in most provinces in Canada. Rum-running—smuggling liquor across the border—was big business until 1933, when the U.S. government repealed Prohibition.

A Rose by Any Other Name

Canadian bootleg liquor was also known as Moose Milk, Moose Juice and Bathtub Gin.

The Real McCoy

Bill McCoy was a boat builder from Nova Scotia who smuggled high-quality liquor into the eastern seaboard states during U.S. Prohibition. His high standards made his name synonymous with authenticity, and he became a wealthy man before he was finally convicted of smuggling.

Illegal Liquor Lexicon

BLIND PIG
The term is not Canadian in origin, but came into general use here during Prohibition. A bootlegger in Massachusetts came up with an inventive way to advertise when sale of hard liquor was prohibited. His sign invited patrons to pay a fee to come in to see a striped pig. Once they paid, the patrons were sent to a room where a glass of illegal liquor was waiting for them beside a small clay pig. Since the pig could not see, no one saw any laws being broken. Hence, blind pig.

BOOTLEGGING
This term, which refers to the illegal sale of alcohol (and, more recently, recordings or movies), originated from pirate smugglers' practice of concealing bottles in their boots.

BOOZE
Another word for liquor, the term has been used in Canada since the early 18th century and is derived from the Middle Dutch verb *busen*, meaning "to drink heavily."

DEAD SOLDIER
A slang term for an empty liquor bottle. So-called because its spirit has left its body.

FIREWATER
A strong alcoholic drink that made imbibers liken its ingestion to drinking flaming liquid.

MOONSHINE
Illegal distilled spirits that were usually brewed by the light of the moon to avoid detection by police.

MOUNTAIN DEW
A term originating in Ireland that referred to homemade liquor. It was imported by Irish immigrants to Canada.

SPEAKEASY
A shop or nightclub that sold illegal liquor during Prohibition. The name reflected the way people passed on information about their locations in low tones to avoid being overheard by police. The term was likely derived from the 19th-century British "speak softly" shops that sold contraband goods.

STILL
A shortened form of the word "distill." It refers to an apparatus used to render alcoholic drinks by distillation.

WINE

Good wine needs no bush, and perhaps products that people
really want need no hard-sell or soft-sell T.V. push.
Why not? Look at pot.*
–Marshall McLuhan (1911–80)

In Vino Veritas?

Although it is a common belief that people tend to tell the truth under the influence of wine, no studies have confirmed this. What has been found is that people tend to say things under the influence that inhibition (and common sense) might prevent them from saying when sober.

*"He was minding his own business when
the wine attacked him..."*
The term "attack" is used in wine-tasting to indicate a wine's initial impact
on the palate.

---

* This is a reference to a line from Shakespeare's *As You Like It,* which harkens back to an old English tradition before signs were common, when people selling wine would plant a bush outside their establishment as a marker. If their wine was good, the word would spread and the bush would no longer be necessary.

Some Canadian Wine History

After Canadian Prohibition ended in 1927, small wine merchants were among the first casualties. Because wine was not prohibited, as beer and hard liquor were, many wineries sprang up in numerous grape-growing areas of Canada. In Ontario alone, 61 wineries were in operation by the late 1920s. When Prohibition was repealed, provincial governments took control of beer and hard liquor production, sales and distribution.

In an attempt to maintain some control over the wineries during this period, the government of Ontario placed a moratorium on new licences to produce and sell wine. The ban remained in place for over four decades, during which time the large wineries based in Ontario absorbed the smaller ones until, in 1974, there were only six left.

At about this time, the Niagara-on-the-Lake wine-growing team of Donald Ziraldo and Karl Kaiser persuaded the Ontario government to grant them a new wine-production licence. Inniskillin Wines was born, paving the way for other small but intrepid wine producers. In the Okanagan Valley of British Columbia, Harry McWatters followed in their footsteps a few years later and opened Sumac Ridge Estate Winery in 1979. The Canadian wine industry was on its way!

DID YOU KNOW?

The VQA (Vintner's Quality Alliance), a regulatory system of standards, was launched in Ontario in 1988. A similar system of VQA was adopted by British Columbia vintners in 1990.

There are four distinct wine-growing regions in Canada: the provinces of Ontario, British Columbia, Nova Scotia and Québec. To date, only Ontario and British Columbia are producing wines to VQA standards.

Pelee Island

Medal-winning wines are produced on the 10-mile long, 3-mile wide island known as Pelee Island. Pelee Island winery is one of the largest grape-growing wineries in Canada—more than 550 acres of laser-straight rows of grapes. The town of Kingsville and Pelee Island were a haven for nature lovers, but now boast high-quality white grape varieties as well as several reds. Lake Erie moderates the climate on the island and provides conditions comparable to the Bordeaux region of France.

Put a Cork (Back) in It!

Vessel stoppers of natural cork were first used by the Greeks and Romans in the 5th century BC. The material came from the renewable bark of the cork oak (*Quercus Super L.*), a tree with a 200-year life expectancy. The natural cork was extremely light, impervious to water and in plentiful and renewable supply in the western Mediterranean areas, particularly Portugal.

Up until the last few years, nearly all wines bottles sold in Canada were stopped with natural cork. The material was in good supply as a result of careful management of cork forests, where virgin cork could, under legislation, be harvested only after a tree was at least 25 years old and then only every 9 to 12 years to allow maintenance of the tree's optimum health. With increasing demand in recent years, legislation of cork harvesting has become more lax. As a result, trees can now be harvested every three or four years. The result is a much inferior cork that can allow air inside wine bottles, which ruins the wine inside.

Canadian wine bottlers have turned to human-made corks, most of them manufactured from ethel-vinyl acetate. While light and impervious to water, they are not biodegradable.

DID YOU KNOW?

Nearly all of the commercial wine produced in Canada comes from Ontario (75 percent) and British Columbia (23 percent). The remaining 2 percent of the domestic commercial wine supply comes from Québec and Nova Scotia.

Cold Comfort

Icewine is a late-harvest sweet dessert wine made from grapes, usually of the thick-skinned Vidal or Riesling variety, that have frozen on the vine and been harvested when temperatures reach –8°C to –10°C. Both Ontario and British Columbia produce excellent icewines.

Marble-ous!

To keep leftover wine from oxidizing, simply fill the less-than-full bottle with marbles to bring the level of the wine as high as possible into the neck, then re-cork it. This will limit the surface of wine exposed to the air, thus reducing the amount of oxidization.

 Canada is considered the producer of the finest icewines in the world.

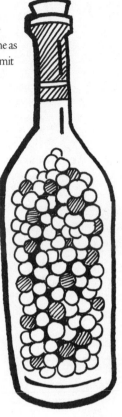

HIC! If Wine is Your Beverage of Choice...

Canada's Opimian Society might be your club of choice. Devoted to the appreciation of wine, the society has operated for more than 30 years and was named for the consul of Rome, Lucius Opimius whose office produced the finest vintage of the Roman Empire. Chapters hold events such as wine tastings, a wine-buying cooperative, wine tours of both new- and old-world wineries as well as educational dinners. Founded in 1973, the society boasts chapters in all regions of the country and is Canada's largest wine club.

SMOKE AND MIRRORS

When the spirit moves them,
they pulverize this herb and place it at one end,
lighting it with a fire brand,
and draw on the other end so long that
they fill their bodies with smoke until it comes out
of their mouth and nostrils as from a chimney.
They claim it keeps them warm and in good health.
They never travel without this herb...

Jacques Cartier, circa 1535

DID YOU  KNOW?

Tobacco, a key element in medicine bundles, was a highly prized product in First Nations cultures. It was essential to ritual and ceremony and was cultivated by many North American aboriginal peoples.

Up in Smoke

It is estimated that more than 45,000 Canadians die each year from disease or illness caused by using tobacco, costing our health care system close to $4 billion dollars annually.

Canada is almost a smoke-free environment. By December 2004, 10 of the 13 provinces and territories had banned smoking in the workplace, including restaurants and bars. Only Québec and the Yukon have not. Many assume these moves will ultimately result in across-Canada ban on smoking in all public places.

No Surprises Here

Canada's proposed ban on smoking shouldn't come as a surprise. King James I, of Mother England, had his own less-than-subtle views on smoking. In 1604 he wrote that it was "a custome lothsome to the eye, hateful to the Nose, harmefull to the braine, dangerous to the Lungs, and the blacke stinking fume thereof, neerest resembling the horrible Stigian smoke of the pit that is bottomelesse."

So Smoke Up, But Save Your Last Butt...

On December 10, 2004, New Zealand became a smoke-free country. The butt of a cigarette smoked in public in the final few seconds before the smoking ban came into effect was originally listed on an internet sale website at $1 NZ. Within days, the bid to beat had risen to $5400 US. You never know how much the last butt in Canada will be worth if this country follows suit.

Tilsonburg, Tilsonburg
My back still aches
when I hear that word...
–Stompin' Tom Connors (1936–)
from "Tilsonburg"

Charles Thomas (Stompin' Tom) Connors, songwriter, guitarist, fiddler, Juno Award-winner and Canadian musical icon, was born in St. John, NB. He had a tough young life, often working long hours at backbreaking jobs, such as picking tobacco in the fields of Tilsonburg. These experiences gave him plenty of material for the lyrics he loved to write. He wrote his first song at the age of 11 and took up guitar at age 15, beginning his professional singing career in 1964 in bars in Timmins, ON, where he had to stomp his booted foot to keep time over the noise in the room. The stomping became a gimmick, earning him the nickname that has made him a household name in Canada.

One look at Reversing Falls, darlin', not far down the road from his Saint John, NB, birthplace, was all that was needed for 11-year-old Tom to put a pen to paper, add a few strums of his guitar and alter his life's path. While the girls were out at Bingo, and the boys were gettin' stinko, young Tom Connors was working his way across this land, until he chanced to stop at a little nickel town on a Sudbury Saturday night. An ode for the road later, with many a Bud the spud under his belt, Tom had stomped his way into Canada's musical heart. Nothing could stop him once he met up with Red River Jane, not even when she called from Montréal. By that time he was long gone to the Yukon. Along the way, he stopped to watch many a good old hockey game, and even when the sound system broke down, you could hear Tom's boot stompin' on the floor to keep the rhythm over the noise of the bars.

Quiz Question
Can you name all the Stompin' Tom song titles or lines from songs embedded in the paragraph above? (HINT: There are 10)

- ☞ Reversing Falls Darling
- ☞ While the girls were out at Bingo, and the boys were gettin' stinko
- ☞ Across This Land
- ☞ Sudbury Saturday Night
- ☞ An Ode For the Road
- ☞ Bud the Spud
- ☞ Red River Jane
- ☞ She Called from Montréal
- ☞ Long Gone to the Yukon
- ☞ Good Old Hockey Game

WILDCAT STRIKES!

If we try to understand and sensibly appreciate Native myth and legend, we must be willing, first of all, to accept that there is involved here a very special way of seeing the world. Secondly, and a necessary further step, we must make an attempt to participate in this way of seeing.

–James Dumont, Anishinaabe scholar

Big Cat

The cougar, also called mountain lion or puma, is the second-largest cat native to the Americas and the fourth-largest cat in the world. It is the largest of the three wild felines native to Canada (the lynx and the bobcat are the other two). The cougar, its name an adaptation of the native Brazilian *cuguacuarana*, was originally called *carcajou* by French-speaking explorers and *pitwal* by the Malechite natives of New Brunswick.

Although once ranging from one coast to the other in Canada, cougars today are common only in the western provinces, most often Alberta and British Columbia. Sporadic sightings continue to be reported in all provinces of Canada except Prince Edward Island.

Nature's Way

Contrary to the modern urban dweller's depiction of most wild animals as vicious, evil and vindictive, aboriginal peoples celebrate and revere even the most dangerous of wild animals as partners in a shared existence.

Don't Take It Personally!

Wild animals do not share the idea that humans are at the top of the food chain or are somehow untouchable. To a hungry meat-eater, a human being fits into the same category as any other item on its list of edibles—we are simply prey.

Since 1987, only three deaths have been attributed to cougar attacks in Canada, and there were only 27 documented cougars attacks in the 20th century. All recorded attacks have been made by very young, underweight or starving animals, or by animals that have been surprised while feeding or caring for young.

DID YOU KNOW?

A cougar runs at average speeds of 35 km/h. It can spring over five metres from a standing position and is capable of killing an animal six times its own weight.

Big Prints—No Cougar!

Several sightings in various eastern locations have caused wildlife management experts to take the eastern cougar off the endangered list and designate this sub-species as "data deficient":

- ☛ In 1991, a family spotted a cougar while they were barbecuing in their backyard near Fredericton, NB.
- ☛ In 1992, a woodsman in Juniper, NB, reported sighting a large cougar. When wildlife experts examined the prints, indicating a stride over a metre long, there was no doubt they had been made by a cougar.
- ☛ In 1993, a woman sighted a large black cougar near her home in Cormierville, NB. The sighting was later confirmed by wildlife biologists, who identified the tracks.
- ☛ In 2003, a Nepean, ON, resident reported sighting a large, light-coloured cougar in a corn field several hundred metres from the boundary of her backyard. Police arrived on the scene minutes after the animal had disappeared into the nearby woods.
- ☛ In 2004, an Ottawa resident reported several sightings of a tan-coloured cougar sunning itself on rocks in one section of the protected Greenbelt region.

The Dunvargon Whooper

Legend has it that the eerie screeches heard in the night near the Dunvargon River in New Brunswick's Miramichi region are the screams of the ghost of a murdered lumberjack who was buried in the area. Area naturalists believe the sounds are made by cougars.

Black Magic!

Close to 40 percent of all reported cougar sightings in New Brunswick describe black cougars. The panther is the only known wild black cat, and it is found exclusively in South America. Wildlife experts suggest that the unique colourations of the sighted cougars may be the result of a genetic anomaly.

How to Escape from a Cougar

If you have followed all the precautions outlined by naturalists to avoid confrontation and still find yourself in a standoff with a cougar, here are a few things you may want to do (or avoid doing):

☞ DO NOT run
☞ Turn to face the animal
☞ Open your coat wide and make yourself appear as large as possible
☞ Remain standing
☞ Back away slowly

If the animal still does not leave, throw stones, wave your arms, and shout in a deep, loud voice. Do not give up even if the animal attacks—you may still survive if you fight back, being careful to protect the back of your neck, the cougar's preferred location for finishing off its victims.

THE WOLVERINE

Picture a weasel...that little demon of destruction, that small atom of insensate courage, that symbol of slaughter, sleeplessness and tireless, incredible activity. Picture that scrap of demoniac fury, multiply that mite some 50 times, and you have the likeness of a wolverine.

–Ernest Thompson Seton (1860–1946)

Ferocious Little Devils

With a reputation for ferocity that far exceeds its size, the wolverine, a member of the weasel family, has been described as the fiercest creature on Earth. Wolverines will travel as much as 40 kilometres in one day in search of food to satisfy their voracious appetites. Although they will hunt if required, they are basically scavengers, aggressive and strong enough to drive large bears away from their kills.

As ferocious as they are, wolverines are rarely encountered by humans in the wild. There are a number of reasons for this:

- Its enormous range, which for males can exceed 1000 square kilometres
- Low population densities
- Wide variations in wolverine habitat

Prize Pelts

Considered one of the most beautiful natural furs, wolverine is a highly prized pelt, selling for an average of $400 if in prime condition. Approximately 500 wolverine pelts are sold in Canada each year, over three-quarters of them coming from British Columbia, Nunavut, Yukon and the Northwest Territories. Wolverines are considered endangered in Québec and Labrador, and "of special concern" in other areas west of Hudson Bay.

The Stuff of Myth and Legend

The wolverine features strongly in native myth and legend and is called by various names: skunk bear, Indian devil, *ommeethatsees* (in Cree), devil bear, hyena of the north and carcajou.*

Feats of Great Strength

During the 1930s in British Columbia, one wolverine, intent on chewing its way into a meat locker, was finally caught in leg-hold traps. It was last seen dragging away a large slab of meat. It had traps attached to three of its legs.

Another wolverine was seen dragging an adult mountain goat several kilometres. Others have been known to carry away entire moose carcasses and caribou heads. These are amazing feats of strength when you consider that the average wolverine weighs about 14 kilograms.

DID YOU  KNOW?

The wolverine bears a strong resemblance to the Tasmanian devil, but is not related to it.

* Carcajou was also the name given to cougars by the French-speaking settlers in New Brunswick. Since both animals are observed to "play" with their kill, the name may have been derived from the French *carcasse* (carcass) and *jouer* (to play).

BEARS

*There are three species of bear native to Canada: the polar bear,
the black bear and the brown bear or grizzly.*

Fatal Bear Attacks Are Rare

Canada's black bear population is about 400,000. In the past 40 years, there have been eight people killed by black bears in Québec and Ontario. The most recent attack in that area was at Valcartier, QC, in July 2000, when Mary Beth Miller, a 24-year-old biathlete doing a lone training run on a groomed trail, was fatally mauled by a black bear. In June 2005, a grizzly bear, which had recently been relocated, returned to Canmore, AB, and attacked and killed a jogger. On August 27, 2005, in Selkirk, MB, 69-year-old Harvey Robinson was picking plums on his farm when a black bear mauled and killed him.

The first recorded sighting of a grizzly bear in Canada by Europeans was in August 1691, when explorer Henry Kelsey wrote about seeing "a great sort of bear" near an area now known as The Pas, MB.

DID YOU KNOW?

Polar bears have the unique ability among bears to slow down their metabolism for long periods at any time of the year if food is scarce. Grizzlies and black bears slow their metabolism during the winter to conserve heat and energy, but at other times of year they will die if food is scarce.

Well...duh!

Some reports suggest that there have been fewer than two dozen fatalities from bear attacks in all of North America in the last 30 years. Human ignorance is at fault in most cases. Here are a few examples of rocket scientists who got away with their lives:

- In 2002, a large group of tourists hiking near Helen Lake, AB, surrounded a grizzly in an attempt to take its picture. The bear charged.
- In 2003, a camper at Canmore, AB, who had eaten part of a hamburger inside his tent and left the meaty garbage next to his bedroll, was incensed when a grizzly swiped a hole in his tent wall during the night.
- In 2004, in Banff, parents smeared honey on their two-year-old child's face, hoping to snap a photo of a black bear licking it off. The parents got a tongue lashing from other tourists, who chased the bear away to keep it from approaching the child.

The Grizzly Truth

- The grizzly's range has dwindled to less than half what it was a century ago due to encroaching human populations.
- Previously found in all areas of Canada, it is now common only in the northwestern regions of northern British Columbia, Yukon, Alaska and Northwest Territories.
- Grizzly bears now number fewer than 30,000 in Canada. Approximately half that population is found in British Columbia.
- Grizzlies are considered to be omnivorous, with only a small percentage of their diet made up of meat. They subsist mostly on berries, roots, shrubs and insects, occasionally supplementing their diets, particularly in springtime, with young mammals or with small rodents and fish.
- Like all bears, grizzlies will make frequent repeat visits to areas where food is easily accessible, such as campgrounds and garbage dumps.

The Bear in Award-Winning CanLit

Bear, by Ontario author Marian Engel (1933–85), is the story of a young woman who moves to a remote island in northern Ontario, where she develops a unique relationship with the island's only other inhabitant, a bear. The novel won the Governor General's Award for fiction in 1976 and was listed by *Quill & Quire* as one of the 40 great Canadian fiction books of the century.

A Famous Bear of Little Brain

Harry Colebourn, a lieutenant with the 2nd Canadian Infantry Brigade, made a stop in White River, ON, on his way to combat posting in Europe during World War I. While in Ontario, he bought a bear cub from a hunter for $20.

The bear, named Winnie after Colebourn's home town of Winnipeg, became his Brigade's mascot overseas. When Colebourn was posted to France, he donated the bear to the London Zoo, where it became a favourite of the son of writer A.A. Milne. Milne adopted the bear as the main character of his series of Winnie-the-Pooh books, the first of which was published in 1926.

Polar Bear Facts

- ☛ The polar bear is the largest land carnivore in the world.
- ☛ Males on average weigh between 400 and 600 kilograms, but some may reach 800 kilograms.
- ☛ Their habitat is generally limited to Arctic coastal areas, where they have ready access to seals, their favourite food.
- ☛ Approximately 30,000 polar bears live wild in the world today, with 50 percent of them in Canada, where they are currently designated as a species of special conservation concern.
- ☛ The polar bear's skin is black, making it better able to absorb the sun's rays and preserve body heat.
- ☛ Despite its appearance, polar bear hair is not white, but translucent, allowing the sun's rays to penetrate deep down to the skin.
- ☛ A polar bear's sense of smell is so acute that it can detect seal breathing holes from a kilometre away, even when they are covered in snow and ice more than 90 centimetres thick.

WARNING

There is no safe distance from a bear. All three Canadian species can outrun and outclimb humans.

Does Your Letter "Bear" a Canadian Stamp?

The $8 stamp, which has the highest face value of Canadian postage, features the grizzly bear. The polar bear appears on the $2 stamp.

Strong Native Symbolism

The bear is a recurrent symbol of strength in aboriginal myth and legend. The National Aboriginal Veterans' Monument in Ottawa features the bear, along with the wolf, the eagle and the elk, standing with human figures representative of aboriginal Canadians who served in our armed forces.

RULE OF THUMB

Although all bears are dangerous, the following three situations should be avoided at all costs:

- Females protecting cubs
- Bears defending a kill
- Bears accustomed to human food

WHEN IN BEAR COUNTRY

- Stay in groups
- Leave your dog at home
- Make plenty of noise
- Keep foods sealed and out of reach (e.g., in your car's trunk)
- Never cook or eat in your tent

IF CONFRONTED BY A BEAR

- Never turn and run
- Remain calm
- Make loud noises or shout
- Back away, avoiding eye contact with the bear
- Provide the bear with an escape route

THE BEAVER

The beaver, which has come to represent Canada
as the eagle does the United States
and the lion Britain,
is a flat-tailed, slow-witted, toothy rodent known to bite off its
own testicles or to stand under its own falling trees.

–June Callwood (1924–)

AUTHOR'S NOTE: The original reference to the beaver biting off his own testicles is attributed to Leonardo da Vinci (1452–1519), but he wasn't Canadian. June Callwood is.

Castor canadiensis, the Canadian beaver, is the largest rodent in North America and has been Canada's official emblem since 1975. The beaver image decorates the Canadian nickel (5¢), is the centrepiece of the Canadian Pacific Railway crest and was featured as Amik, mascot of the 1976 Summer Olympics. Our toothy national animal appeared on the first Canadian postage stamp, the "Threepenny Beaver" issued in 1851.

By the Way...

1. What famous Canadian designed the Threepenny Beaver stamp?

Sir Sanford Fleming (1827–1915)

2. What is Sir Sanford Fleming best known for?

He was the Scottish-born Canadian engineer who designed Universal Standard Time, which was put into worldwide use in 1884.

...Speaking of Stamps

If you are a member of BNAPS (British North American Philatelic Society) and you prove yourself worthy, you may be inducted into its honorary fellowship, the Order of the Beaver.

The Good, the Bad and the Ugly

Although somewhat homely and in need of cosmetic dentistry, the beaver was, at one time, the mainstay of Canada's fur trade and the catalyst for much of Canada's early exploration and settlement.

Hot Commodity

Beginning in the 1600s, with the arrival of the first beaver pelts from Canada, stylish European men and women developed a great liking for hats made of felt from the lightweight yet warm beaver fur. Since only the underlayers of fur were used in the hat-making process, beaver was sold by the pound rather than by the pelt, and it became by far the most expensive and sought-after Canadian natural product. At the height of its popularity, one beaver skin was equal in value to five red fox skins or 45 muskrat skins!

DID YOU KNOW?

Young beavers are called kits.

Beaver Preserves

In the middle of the 19th century, European fashion changed, and demand for beaver declined, but damage to the beaver population had already been done. By the early 1930s, the beaver was almost extinct. The Québec government created beaver preserves and made it illegal to trap beaver until the population grew to a desired level.

Annual kill quotas were set up, and the government distributed brass beaver tokens to encourage growth of the beaver population. For every beaver living on their property, landowners received one token. Tokens became legal tender. Less than 15 years after the program began, the beaver population had risen to 1300. Beavers are again plentiful and are found in every Canadian province.

DID YOU KNOW?

Beaver dams act as sediment traps and stabilize the flow of streams. Flooded ponds provide habitat for many species of wildlife and offer a safe location where other animals can hide during forest fires.

Beaver Tails

The next time a tourist asks you if beaver is part of the Canadian diet, you can answer "Yes, but only the tail!" In 1980, Grant and Pam Hooker introduced a new treat called Beaver Tails in Ottawa's Byward Market district.

Today, people in 130 venues around the world, including the Canada Pavilion at Walt Disney World's Epcot Centre in Orlando, Florida, can enjoy the delectable hot pastries. Based on a traditional voyageur recipe, Beaver Tails are made with whole wheat flour, formed into shapes resembling a beaver's tail, then deep-fried and sprinkled with any number of toppings, including the perennial favourite, brown sugar and cinnamon.

I have found that in the beaver, with its almost human,
very nearly child-like appeal,
I had seized on a powerful weapon.
Placed in the vanguard,
the beaver constituted the thin edge of the wedge.
–Grey Owl (1888–1938)

Grey Owl

In part, the concern over the dwindling beaver population was a result of the writings of the author and adventurer who called himself Grey Owl. Archie Belaney was born in England in 1888, where he developed a love for playing Cowboys and Indians.

At the age of 18, he immigrated to Canada and lived for some time in northern Ontario and Québec, where he learned to hunt, fish and trap. For the rest of his life he passed himself off as Métis, living off the land in various wilderness locations in Canada.

He began writing books that encouraged wildlife conservation, among them *Adventures of Sajo and Her Beaver People*, which was published in 1935. He finally settled in northern Saskatchewan, where he died in 1938 at the age of 50.

WARNING

Do not try to outswim a beaver. When alarmed, it can reach speeds up to 7 km/h in the water, and its bite could inflict severe damage.

Flying Beavers?

The de Havilland Beaver, developed in the 1940s, can take off from, and land on, water, snow or land. Although out of production since 1967, two-thirds of the 1692 craft built are still flying.

DID YOU KNOW?

One adult beaver cuts down an average of 216 trees per year. A lone beaver can fell a tree as large as 40 centimetres in diameter.

Quiz Question

What type of plane was used in the beach scenes for the Hollywood movie *Six Days and Seven Nights*, starring Harrison Ford and Anne Heche?

You guessed it, a de Havilland Beaver.

ON THE HOOF
Of Moose and Men

There are five species of ungulates (hooved animals) native to Canada: bison, moose, North American elk, deer and caribou. Although the various species are found in different areas, the survival of aboriginal groups has traditionally been closely tied to ungulate populations.

Caribou

Three subspecies of caribou, known as *tuk-tu* in Inuktitut, are found in Canada. Woodland caribou are found in the Cordilleras. They tend to stay in smaller herds and travel over shorter distances than the other subspecies. The woodland caribou population has been dwindling since the beginning of the 20th century, and they were added to Alberta's endangered wildlife list in 1985.

Barren ground caribou are found in the Arctic regions. Migrating over long, predictable routes, this is the most numerous of the subspecies. It provided aboriginal people with a source of meat for food, skins for clothing and bones for tools.

Peary caribou, also an endangered subspecies, are sometimes seen on islands in the Hudson Strait, but generally remain in tundra areas in summer, then migrate to muskeg and coniferous forests during the winter. Their numbers have decreased significantly, and the subspecies is near extinction.

DID YOU  **KNOW?**

It is illegal to hunt caribou in Alberta.

Uplifting Idea

Although the caribou is much smaller than the moose, its feet are almost the same size as its larger cousin's. The spreadable foot works like a natural snowshoe, giving the caribou an advantage when walking on deep snow and allowing it to eat tree lichen, its primary winter food, which would otherwise be too high to reach.

What a Load!

A large pile of caribou droppings, nearly 3 metres high and more than 800 metres long, was discovered by hikers in the Yukon in 2004. Scientists, who later discovered Stone Age tools and weapons in the dung heap, believe it had been frozen for thousands of years and was only exposed during a particularly warm summer.

Gender Equality

Both male and female caribou carry antlers.

Moose

The largest member of the deer family, an adult bull moose can weigh as much as 800 kilograms, although they average around 600 kilograms. Moose are very much at home in the water. Powerful swimmers, they are able to dive 5 metres or more in search of tender shoots at the bottom of a pond or lake.

Deer

There are several subspecies of deer in Canada, including white-tailed deer, black-tailed deer and mule deer.

Fresh as a Baby!

A fawn does not give off any odour, a condition that protects it from being preyed upon in the wild when the doe is away for long periods of time, foraging for food.

DID YOU KNOW?

Deer reproduce quickly. A healthy herd can double its population in one good year.

Elk (Wapiti)

The North American elk, also known as the wapiti, is second in size only to the moose. An adult bull elk stands about 150 centimetres tall at the shoulder and weighs about 300 to 350 kilograms, although some large bulls approach 500 kilograms in late summer before the breeding season.

There are currently over 70,000 elk in Canada, with almost half the population living in the Kootenay region of British Columbia. The remaining numbers are spread across Alberta (20,000), Saskatchewan (15,000) and Manitoba (7000).

Annual Event

Elk horns are shed in the fall and grow new each year.

Bison

Two subspecies of bison exist in Canada today—the wood bison and the plains bison. Now considered a threatened species, 30 to 70 million of these magnificent creatures once roamed North America, the average male standing 2 metres high and weighing close to 1000 kilograms.

Bison are known for longevity, often living as long as 40 years, but they were decimated during the 1800s and early 1900s by European settlers who killed them for their hides and trophy skulls.

Back from Extinction

Thought to be nearly extinct in the 1940s as a result of interbreeding with the plains bison, a herd of pure wood bison was found in the late 1950s. Several of them were captured and released in the Mackenzie Bison Sanctuary in Alberta, where they have increased their numbers to a stable population of more than 2000.

The bison is the largest land animal in North America, and the largest herd of free-ranging wood bison in the world is in the Mackenzie Bison Sanctuary in Alberta.

Bison can distinguish smells from a distance of three kilometres and can run at speeds up to 50 km/h.

Spirit of Peace

In May 2005, a rare white bison, christened Spirit of Peace, was born on the Blatz Bison Ranch in the North Peace country at Fort St. John, BC. A one in a million occurrence, the white bison is said to be a sacred symbol of hope and unity for First Nations people. Although the baby, born prematurely, died after six and a half weeks, the spirit of hope that accompanied her birth remains.

SNAKES ALIVE!

...the small snake gathered glidingly and slid,
but with such cadence to its rapt advance
that when it stopped once more to raise its head
it was stiller than the stillest mineral,
and when it moved again it moved the way
a curl of water slips along a stone
or like the ardent progress of a tear
till deeper still it gave the rubbled grass
and the dull hollows where its ripple ran
lithe scintillas of exuberance...

–Eric Ormsby (1941–)

from "Garter Snake"

Eric Ormsby, a Canadian citizen born in Atlanta, GA, and educated at Princeton, took a post as professor of Near Eastern studies at McGill University in the mid-1980s. His poetry, much of it reflecting his love of nature, was first published when Ormsby was nearly 50 and has appeared in the *Norton Anthology of Poetry* and in the *New Yorker* magazine.

The largest of Canada's 25 snake species are southern Ontario's black rat snakes, which have reached lengths of 2.57 metres. Average size is 1.5 to 1.8 metres. Although non-venomous and harmless to humans, they may rear and strike if threatened, vibrating their tails in imitation of rattlesnakes.

Black rat snakes have been in Canada for more than 7000 years, but their habitats are decreasing every year. Only two isolated populations are known in Canada today.

Number of Snake Species by Province (per Family)

PROVINCE	BOAS	PIT VIPERS	COLUBRIDS[*]
British Columbia	1	1	7
Alberta	0	1	5
Saskatchewan	0	1	8
Manitoba	0	0	5
Ontario	0	2	14
Québec	0	0	7
New Brunswick	0	0	4
Nova Scotia	0	0	5
Prince Edward Island	0	0	3
Newfoundland/Labrador	no snakes		
Yukon	no snakes		
Northwest Territories	0	0	1
Nunavut	no snakes		

* So-called typical snakes, including milk snakes, garter snakes, green snakes, etc.

It's Mine! No, It's Mine. I'd Know that Tongue Anywhere!

In summer 2003, a live, 50-centimetre, orange-and-black tropical corn snake was found sunning itself on a sidewalk in Winnipeg. Described in the newspapers as cute and friendly with a penchant for gently licking human faces, it was claimed by several people before finally being returned to its rightful owner.

Size Really Doesn't Matter

The size of the snake has nothing to do with the amount of venom in its bite.

Bites from young venomous snakes are usually deadlier than bites from adults because young snakes tend to bite deeper and harder.

Reptile Remedy

In Canada's early history, aboriginals used echinacea, derived from the purple cone flower, as a remedy for snake bites.

The Snakepits of Narcisse

Just off Highway 17 north of Narcisse, MB, you might see the largest collection of snakes you will ever witness in the wild. Every spring, the four limestone snake dens are host to tens of thousands of red-sided garter snakes as they gather for the spring mating ritual.

In the mating ritual, which occurs between late April and mid-May, males emerge first from their winter sleep and wait for the larger females to show themselves. As each female emerges, she is surrounded by several males, who twine themselves around her, forming a "mating ball," which can then be seen slithering along the ground.

Adult snakes will usually return to the same overwintering den from year to year, using scent trails to find their way. Some will find warmth and security in sheds and barns; others, to the consternation of some people in the area, will find their way into homes, where they will sleep soundly throughout the winter.

Quiz Question

What is ophidiophobia?

A morbid fear of snakes.

Annual Guests

Jim and Johanna Rodger of Argyle, MB, have an ongoing relationship with the snakes that find their way into their rural home every fall. "They're clean; they don't bother us; and they keep down the rodent population," says Jim. "We don't mind them at all," adds Johanna, "but the numbers are becoming a little overwhelming."

In spring 2005, they transported over 1700 snakes from their basement, and another 500 from their septic field, to some limestone quarries sufficiently distant to discourage them from returning every year. The snakes, it seems, have other ideas!

DID YOU KNOW?

Snakes have neither eyelids nor ear holes. Their forked tongues are equipped with a type of radar that allows them to follow scent trails.

Night Moves

A permanent population of night snakes (*Hypsiglena torquata*), a nocturnal member of the viper family of poisonous snakes, has been found in the lower Okanagan Valley of British Columbia. The night snake's venom, although toxic to lizards and frogs, is believed to be harmless to humans. "Believed to be" may be small comfort for anyone inclined to take nighttime walks in the snake's neighbourhood.

The Boa Facts

Canada's only boa constrictor is the rubber boa, a small (less than one metre long) non-venomous snake, native to the southwestern section of British Columbia's Kootenay National Park.

DID YOU KNOW?

The vast majority of snake bites that occur in Canada are from exotic snakes kept in zoos or as pets in private homes.

Quiz Question
What is ophiolatry?

The worship of snakes

Rare and Colourful

Georges Island and McNab Island, both in Halifax Harbour, are home to peculiar-looking black garter snakes. At first people thought they were escaped tropical snakes and feared that they were poisonous. On investigation, wildlife experts have discovered that the snakes are melanistic (black pigmented) and are products of a genetic aberration that is likely caused, at least in part, by inbreeding.

Eastern Massasauga Rattler

The Massasauga Rattler, a pit viper on the Canadian Endangered Species List, has been hunted relentlessly. With its diamond-shaped head and vertical pupils, it is so distinct that it is an easy target for people who seem inclined to eliminate it, even though there have only been two recorded deaths from rattlesnake bites in Eastern Canada. The one other pit viper in Ontario is the Timber Rattlesnake, which has been all but eradicated in most areas.

ON THE WING

There's a bluebird on my windowsill,
there's a rainbow in the sky.
There are happy songs your heart can sing,
they're enough to make you sigh.

–Elizabeth Clarke (1911–60)
from "Bluebird on My Windowsill"

Country Bluebird

The Rhythm Pals, a country vocal group from New Westminster, BC, that was popular during the 1940s and 1950s, were the first to record "Bluebird on My Windowsill." The song was written in 1948 by Carmen Elizabeth Clarke, a nurse who was inspired when a bird perched on a windowsill of the Hospital for Sick and Crippled Children in Vancouver, where she was working. It was recorded by many famous artists, including Doris Day, who made it a hit in 1949.

Canada's smallest bird, the calliope hummingbird (*Stellula calliope*), is 7 centimetres in length, on average, and weighs approximately 25 grams. It is native to the interior of British Columbia and the mountain areas of southwestern Alberta.

Canada's largest bird is the bald eagle, with an average wingspan of about 2 metres and average weight of more than 7 kilograms. It breeds from coast to coast in Canada, with the largest populations in the northern boreal forests and coastal regions of British Columbia.

DID YOU KNOW?

Hummingbirds have the unique ability among birds to fly forward or backward or to hover in one spot. They are capable of wing speeds of 55 to 75 beats per second.

The largest concentration of bald eagles in the world is located in the area around Squamish, BC, where 1942 mature eagles and their offspring were tallied in the 2001 count. The average annual count is about 1700 eagles.

DID YOU KNOW?

The eagle feather symbolizes spiritual strength in aboriginal cultures and is a sacred object. The homage First Nations people give to the eagle feather is their way of showing respect for ancestors, for themselves and for Native culture.

Monumental

Three of the largest Canada goose statues in the world can be seen just off the Trans-Canada Highway at Wawa, ON. *Wawa* is the Ojibway word for goose.

Canada's largest butterfly is the monarch, with a wingspan of 9.5 centimetres. Canada's smallest butterfly is the bog elfin, with a wingspan of 1.5 centimetres.

Good Luck Times Two

In Maritime folklore, it is good fortune if two black crows fly over your head, but very bad luck if there is only one.

Pheathered Phrases

The expression "to eat crow" was coined during the American invasion of Canada in the War of 1812. An American soldier who had come across the border in search of food was forced by a British soldier, at gunpoint, to eat part of a crow he had caught before being set free.

The origin of the term "stool pigeon" is a sad story. Hunters of the past used to tie one pigeon to a stool, knowing its cries would attract other pigeons within shooting range. By the middle of the 19th century, passenger pigeons were extinct in the wild in Canada. The last passenger pigeon in the world died in captivity in a Cincinnati zoo on September 1, 1914.

Avian Groupies

A murder of crows

A dole of doves

A charm of finches

A covey of grouse

A cast of hawks

A siege of herons

A exaltation of larks

A tiding of magpies

A sord of mallard

A richesse of martens

A gaggle of geese
(in the air: a skein)

A parliament of owls

A nye of pheasants

A kit of pigeons (in the air)

A stand of plovers

A drift of quail

An unkindness of ravens

A host of sparrows

A murmuration of starlings

A flight of swallows

A lamentation of swans
(in the air, a wedge)

We Love Our Birds

In 2004, consumption of poultry in Canada
was 13.5 kilograms/person.

Bird-Dogs

Vancouver International Airport and Cold Lake Air Force base in Cold Lake, AB,
are two of the airports in Canada using trained border collies to herd birds and
keep them off runways. Many air accidents have been caused by bird encounters,
most of which occurred when a large bird was sucked into the engine on take-off.

LARGER THAN LIFE

There were giants in the earth in those days;
and also after that,
when the sons of God came in unto the daughters of men,
and they bore children to them,
the same became mighty men which were of old, men of renown.
–The Bible, Genesis 6:4

The Gentle Giant: Edouard Beaupré (1881–1902)

Joseph Edouard Beaupré was born in Willow Bunch, SK, to a French-Canadian father and a Métis mother. Born with a malfunctioning pituitary gland, Edouard weighed over five kilograms at birth. By the time he was 11, he was taller than his father. A skilled hunter and rider, Edouard was also highly intelligent and could speak Cree, English, Sioux and French when still very young. His dream to become a rodeo star was shattered when he grew too big to ride even the largest horses. At 17, he was 2.5 metres tall and weighed 140 kilo-grams. Ridiculed in public and ostracized by society, there was little left for him but the circus.

While touring with Barnum & Bailey Circus through-out the United States, Edouard developed tuberculosis and died in 1902, never having thought of himself as anything other than a freak. But his death at age 24 was not the end of his humiliation.

His parents, too poor to have his body returned to Saskatchewan, gave Barnum & Bailey permission to dispose of his remains. Instead of giving Edouard a decent burial, the circus embalmed his body and put it on display. The body was subsequently sold to a department store in the United States and exhibited, naked, in a store window. From there, his body was purchased by anatomy department at the University of Montréal, where it was kept "for research purposes" for 82 years.

In 1975, some of Edouard's relatives discovered, to their horror, what had happened to Edouard's body. They began a long battle with the university to reclaim the body, a battle they finally won in 1989. The family immediately had his remains cremated and returned to his birthplace in Saskatchewan so that he could finally rest in peace.

 Edouard Beaupré was the tallest Canadian in history.

The Cape Breton Giant: Angus McAskill (1825–63)

Angus McAskill was born in the Scottish Hebrides and moved with his parents to St. Ann's, NS, while still a small child. He didn't stay small for long. Of normal size at birth, he began a growth spurt in his teens. By the time he was in his 20s, he was 2.36 metres tall and weighed over 190 kilograms. His hands measured 20 by 30 centimetres. He spent several years touring with travelling sideshows throughout the western hemisphere and was featured for his amazing feats of strength. He returned to Cape Breton in 1853, where he ran a business until his death. He is reportedly the tallest non-pathological (genetically normal) giant in the world.

Big Scorers

☞ Jerry Sokoloski (1983–) of Toronto is Canada's tallest basketball player. At 2.26 metres, he was the tallest player in the NBA's 2004 draft, though no team signed him.

☞ Merlelynn Lange-Harris (1969–), Toronto-born basketball centre, is the tallest woman in Canadian sport at 1.97 metres. She competed for Canada in the 1996 Olympics in Atlanta.

MEDIA AND PUBLISHING

I see Canada as a country torn between a very northern, rather extraordinary, mystical spirit, which it fears, and its desire to present itself to the world as a Scotch banker.

–Robertson Davies (1913–95)

Governor General's Literary Award

Lord Tweedsmuir, Canada's Governor General from 1935 until his death on February 11, 1940, was not only a well-known author and a peer of the British realm. He was also a leader in the move to have Canada develop a distinct identity. Buchan's novels were widely popular, and many expressed an empathy with the people of Canada. His most famous suspense novel, *The Thirty-Nine Steps*, was made into a film of the same name by Alfred Hitchcock.

Lord Tweedmsuir and his wife, the former Susan Grosvenor, also an author, were instrumental in supporting literacy throughout Canada and in building the first library at Rideau Hall.

In 1936, Lord Tweedsmuir created the Governor General's Literary Awards. Seventy years later, these awards continue to be Canada's most prestigious recognition of literary merit.

Recent Winners of the Governor General's Literary Awards

2004
FICTION Miriam Toews
POETRY Roo Borson
DRAMA Morris Panych
NONFICTION Lt.-Gen. Roméo Dallaire
CHILDREN'S (TEXT) Kenneth Oppel
CHILDREN'S (ILLUSTRATION) Stéphane Jorisch
TRANSLATION Judith Cowan

2003
FICTION Douglas Glover
POETRY Tim Lilburn
DRAMA Vern Thiessen
NONFICTION Margaret MacMillan
CHILDREN'S (TEXT) Glen Huser
CHILDREN'S (ILLUSTRATION) Allen Sapp
TRANSLATION Jane Brierley

2002
FICTION Gloria Sawai
POETRY Roy Miki
DRAMA Kevin Kerr
NONFICTION Andrew Nikiforuk
CHILDREN'S (TEXT) Martha Brooks
CHILDREN'S (ILLUSTRATION) Wallace Edward
TRANSLATION Nigel Spencer

2001
FICTION Richard B. Wright
POETRY George Elliott Clarke
DRAMA Kent Stetson
NONFICTION Thomas Homer-Dixon
CHILDREN'S (TEXT) Arthur Slade
CHILDREN'S (ILLUSTRATION) Mireille Levert
TRANSLATION Fred. A. Reed and David Homel

2000
FICTION Michael Ondaatje
POETRY Don McKay
DRAMA Timothy Findley
NONFICTION Nega Mezlekia
CHILDREN'S (TEXT) Deborah Ellis
CHILDREN'S (ILLUSTRATION) Marie-Louise Gay
TRANSLATION Robert Majzels

1999
FICTION Matt Cohen
POETRY Jan Zwicky
DRAMA Michael Healy
NONFICTION Marq de Villiers
CHILDREN'S (TEXT) Rachna Gilmore
CHILDREN'S (ILLUSTRATION) Gary Clement
TRANSLATION Patricia Claxton

The oldest newspaper in Canada, the *Halifax Gazette*, printed its first issue on March 23, 1752.

Fiddle-dee-dee!

The Fiddlehead, a quarterly publication of the University of New Brunswick, is Canada's longest-lasting literary journal, first published in 1945.

Winter Counts

First Nations people of the Canadian Plains did not have an alphabet or a written language until the 19th century. Events of the year were recorded in pictures drawn on buffalo hide. Called "winter counts," they were a way of keeping track of how many winters had passed.

The *Toronto Star* is Canada's largest daily newspaper with a total weekly readership of over 2.5 million.

Reader Decline

There are 102 daily newspapers published in Canada today. That number has not fluctuated by more than six in the last 25 years. Total circulation of daily newspapers decreased from some 5.4 million in 1980 to 4.9 million in 2003.

Lit Support

Anne Gibbons Wilkinson (1910–61), Toronto poet and patron of the arts, published her first book, *Counterpoint to Sleep*, in 1951. She was one of the founders of *The Tamarack Review*. A leading Canadian literary journal during the period of its publication, from 1956 to 1982, *The Tamarack Review* published such distinguished Canadian authors as Mordecai Richler, Margaret Atwood, Timothy Findley and Alice Munro.

Not Talking 'Bout My Generation

I speak for myself, not for a generation. I never have.

–Douglas Coupland (1961–)

Douglas Coupland, artist, designer, sculptor and writer, was credited with coining the widely used term "Generation X." Coupland was born on a Canadian Armed Forces base at Baden-Sollingen, Germany, and grew up in Vancouver. A widely travelled, self-admitted eccentric who refuses to own furniture, Coupland has repeatedly refused to be viewed as the spokesperson for his generation. He has won two Canadian National Awards for Excellence in Design, has published 20 novels and is a regular contributor to such stellar publications as the *New York Times* and *ArtForum*.

MONEY

*We will do our best to spread the wealth of Ontario
across our country.*

–Robert Bourassa (1933–96), former premier of Québec

Up To Their Ears and Beyond

Research by the Vanier Institute of the Family, an Ottawa-based charitable organization, found that the average household in Canada is in debt for 121 percent of its disposable income.

Bytown's Big Pig

The Royal Canadian Mint in Ottawa is
home to the world's largest
piggy bank, 6 metres long
and 4.2 metres high.

Where Could You Get a Deal Like This?

Former Governor General Adrienne Clarkson and her husband, John Ralston Saul, paid $2.74 million for Lester Pearson's former house (read "mansion") in the Annex district of Toronto. The house has nine bedrooms, seven bathrooms, a coach house and annual taxes of just $12,000.

Speaking of Mansions...

According to our national tax agency Conrad Black (aka Lord Black) and his wife, Barbara Amiel, owed $13 million in back taxes to this country's coffers by 2004. Their property in the Kensington neighbourhood of London (England) was sold in early 2005 for a reported $35.4 million dollars, netting Conrad and Barbara a couple of million more than what they paid for it ($32.3 million). The 12,390-square-foot, cream-coloured mansion has seven bedrooms, four bathrooms, five reception areas, an elevator, a cathedral-ceilinged dining room, a swimming pool as well as a plunge pool, a gymnasium and steam room. It makes the GG's digs sound like a low-priced rental.

Sparklingly Canadian

Canada's diamond industry is the third largest in the world, after those in Botswana and Russia. Canada's northern mines now produce close to 14 million carats per year.

Canadians—as obsessed about gas prices as they are about their cars!

- 85 percent remember exactly what they paid for gas on their last fill-up.
- 10 percent are willing to stay in line for 30 minutes for a $0.20/litre discount.
- 43 percent of women and 29 percent of men have eavesdropped to hear about a discount gas spot.
- 30 percent of drivers have stopped for less than $5.00 worth of gas.
- 10 percent of drivers in Manitoba and Saskatchewan have stopped to put less than $2.00 worth of gas in their vehicles.

$$$$

According to Industry Canada, about 2 percent of all Canadians (about 700,000 people) are currently classified as millionaires. Ninety thousand of those are multi-millionaires, worth more than $10 million.

Of Course It's REAL Money—
I Got It at the Bank!

In early 2005, four patrons got an odd assortment of bills when they used the automated teller machines in Riverview, NB. Instead of bills issued by the Royal Canadian Mint, they got Canadian Tire money in denominations ranging from $0.10 to $2.00. No reports on when Canadian Tire will start issuing real money.

The first oil well in North America was drilled at a community 35 kilometres south of Sarnia, ON, in 1858. The town that sprang up around the oil fields was named Oil Springs.

DID YOU KNOW?

Retailers in Canada are not required to accept pennies in payment for any item costing more than $0.50.

NOT-SO-FAMOUS PEOPLE

Legal Cat House

René Chartrand is the keeper of the largest legalized cat house in Canada. It not only sits in the shadow of Ottawa's Peace Tower, but is also on federal property. Mr. Chartrand, in his 80s, has built a sanctuary for stray cats in the city, having inherited the volunteer job in 1987 when the previous caring human died. A retired house painter, Chartrand built a house for his feline guests, a large, cozy structure reflecting the architecture of the nearby Parliament Buildings. Often making them home-cooked meals, he feeds and cares for the cats with his own money and with donations given by kindly folks who visit.

The Canadian–Old Dutch Connection

Maude E. Sutherland, young daughter of a Pictou, NS doctor, is credited with designing the famous logo of a little white-bonneted girl on the Old Dutch Cleanser cans. Around 1907, the American-based Old Dutch company ran a logo contest, open to residents of Canada and the United States. Maude's submission won.

There is an unsubstantiated rumour that American Georgia O'Keeffe was one of the professional artists hired to depict the short-listed entries for presentation to the panel of judges. It is believed that some of the artists' proofs are still in circulation.

Dutch Girl Muse

When she wrote her 1985 novel *The Handmaid's Tale*, Margaret Atwood modelled the uniforms of the handmaids on the clothing of the little Dutch girl on the can. Apparently the image with the hidden face had haunted the author since childhood.

As a child, Canadian poet P.K. Page was also fascinated by the Dutch girl's "picture within a picture within a picture" on the Old Dutch Cleanser can. The impact of the image on her seven-year-old mind was the central theme of the poem "A Backwards Journey," which appears in her 1997 volume *The Hidden Room: Collected Poetry*.

Jerome of Alphonse de Clare

On the cool, sunny morning of September 8, 1863, a lone man was found on a beach near Sandy Cove in the Bay of Fundy off Nova Scotia's northwest coast. Semi-conscious, the man was in a bad state. Within his reach were a jug of water and a tin of biscuits.

His clothing, his appearance and his soft, unscarred hands suggested that he was a gentleman. He was suffering from exposure and cold, but worse, he was in pain from having his legs cut off. Judging from the condition of the stumps, those who found him concluded that his legs had been skillfully amputated not long before he was found, for the wounds had not completely healed.

His rescuers carried him to a nearby village, where the inhabitants agreed to care for him until he recovered. He remained in the village of Alphonse de Clare for nearly 50 years, cared for by a local family and embraced as part of the community, until his death in 1912.

Throughout that time, the man, who had murmured the name "Jerome" in his delirium while on the beach, remained silent. Despite attempts by local people to find out anything about him, even what language he spoke, the mystery of his identity has never been solved.

Canada's Illustrious Illustrated Man

(This story rightfully belongs in a chapter titled "Really Stupid Ideas")

Brent Moffat of Winnipeg, MB, proves there's no limit to what people will do for attention. In 2004, in an attempt to earn a spot in the *Guinness Book of World Records*, he had his body pierced with 5100 needles.

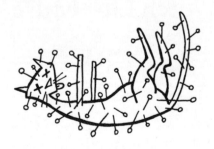

CLEARLY CANADIAN

...BEING A COLLECTION OF CANADIAN MISCELLANY

"I'm going out to flood the rink."
Lucien Rivard

Lucien Rivard apparently used this ruse to get himself outside the locked doors of Montreal's Bordeaux Jail, where he was serving time on drug offences. On March 2, 1965, Rivard abandoned his oh-so-Canadian pursuit of flooding the prison's outdoor hockey rink and scampered over the wall to freedom.

Speaking of Hockey

You have to be pretty big in Canada to spawn a language all your own, and no one can deny that Tim Hortons is BIG! The company was started by former Canadian hockey great Tim Horton (1930–74), born Miles Gilbert Horton in Cochrane, ON. In the midst of a successful hockey career that spanned nearly three decades, Tim Horton opened a small coffee and doughnut shop in Hamilton, ON, in 1964. Named three times to the NHL's All-Star team, Horton was killed in an automobile accident in 1974. His business partner, Ron Joyce, expanded operations of the coffee shop, and today there are more than 2350 Tim Hortons outlets in Canada, with another 230 in the United States.

Coffee Talk, Tim Hortons Style

DOUBLE-DOUBLE = 2 CREAMS, 2 SUGARS

TRIPLE-TRIPLE = 3 CREAMS, 3 SUGARS

FOUR-BY-FOUR = 4 CREAMS, 4 SUGARS

In 2004, the average Canadian drank 93.7 litres of coffee. And thanks in part to the Tim-Speak ease of saying double-double, triple-triple and so on, that average Canadian consumed 1.9 litres of table cream to go along with it.

 Tim Hortons is the largest doughnut and coffee chain in Canada.

Coffee, Tea or...?

In Canada, 97 percent of tea consumed is drunk hot; in the United States, 85 percent of tea is served iced.

D'You Know Juno?

The name of Canada's answer to the the Grammys has two namesakes—Pierre Juneau, first chairman of the Canadian Radio-television and Telecommunications Commission, and Juno, chief goddess of the Roman pantheon. The molten glass and silver-plated aluminum statuettes are awarded annually to deserving Canadian musicians. The award, first presented in 1970, was originally made of walnut and called the Gold Leaf Award. The following year it was renamed to honour Juneau, who enacted the Canadian Content rules, which stipulate the percentage of Canadian content (currently 35 percent) that Canadian radio stations are required to air.

 The first bonspiel in Canada was played on the Don River in Toronto on February 12, 1839. The first Canadian curling club was established in Montréal in 1807.

A Whole New Language!

In curling, you have to know what the skip is saying before you can act:

"Clean"
STAY WITH THE ROCK AND BE READY TO SWEEP

"Never"
LEAVE THE ROCK ALONE

"Hurry hard"
SWEEP AS HARD AS POSSIBLE

DID YOU  KNOW?

Fifteen million Canadians own cellphones.

Phone and Clone

Canadians love their cellphones, but they may be bad news for Canadian men wishing to become fathers. A recent study has shown that male cellphone users who keep their phones on "standby" for most of the day may have reduced sperm counts, in addition to a lower percentage of motile sperm.

- Thirteen-year-old Canadian girls are the most likely in the world to spend more than three hours each day in front of a computer screen
- The average Canadian child watches between two and four hours of television every day.
- Fewer than 50 percent of Canadian kids meet Health Canada guidelines that recommend between 30 and 60 minutes of moderate to vigorous daily exercise.

War Averted!

In 2005, French fries from the McCain Company in New Brunswick saved the day for a Brussels festival featuring *moule frites,* Belgium's most popular food combo of mussels and fries. When the French-speaking Walloon organizers insisted that half the potatoes for the fries had to come from French-speaking farms, the Dutch-speaking Flemish organizers reacted angrily. The festival was saved by a quick-thinking government minister who promptly placed an order with the Canadian company McCain's.

MADE IN
Canada

McCain's is the world's largest supplier of French fries, producing over one million fries per hour.

Poutine

A clearly Canadian take on the old French fry is a concoction called "poutine." Ordinary fries become extraordinary when sprinkled with cheese curds, then smothered in hot gravy. And if you want to sound like a real Québécois(e), do not pronounce this delectable as "poo-teen." In the vernacular it is pronounced "poot-sinn," with the emphasis on the last syllable.

Just the Fats Please!

- ☞ Canada ranks fifth in the world for its percentage of overweight children (ages 10 to 16).
- ☞ Queen's University research for the World Health Organization's 2001–02 study found that 19.3 percent of this country's children are overweight, and 4.1 percent are obese.
- ☞ Malta, at 7.9 percent, has the highest child obesity rate and the highest proportion (25.4 percent) of overweight children in the world.

☞ The United States comes in second, with a 6.8 percent obesity rate and 25.1 percent overweight.

☞ Lithuania has the leanest youth population, with obesity at only 0.4 percent and overweight at 5.1 percent.

More Fat Facts

☞ In 1978–79, 3 percent of children aged 2 to 17 were obese. By 2004, 8 percent were obese.

☞ In 1978–79, the adult obesity rate was 14 percent. In 2005, 25 percent of adults were obese.

☞ The number of calories consumed by Canadians rose by 18 per cent from 1992 to 2002. The proportion of calories from protein, fat and carbohydrates remains fairly constant.

☞ St. Catharines is Canada's fattest city—57.3 percent of adults are overweight or obese. Regina and Saint John, N.B. Windsor and London are close runnersup.

☞ Prince Edward Island is Canada's "fattest" province, with 57 percent of its population overweight.

☞ A child with obese parents has an 80 percent chance of becoming obese.

VARIOUS AND SUNDRY EXTRAS

Just Who is Flying This Thing?

About two percent of all commercial landings in Canada are handled by computerized onboard electronic pilot. All others are done the good old-fashioned way.

Amusing Muses

Emily Carr (1871–1945) British Columbia artists famous for her impressions in oil of West Coast Native totem poles, had a quirky side. While running a boarding house in Victoria to support her art, she surrounded herself with animals. Among the pets of her acquaintance were a cockatoo, a parrot, various dogs, a white rat and a monkey named Woo that she often wheeled about town in a baby carriage.

DID YOU KNOW?

Animals depicted on totem poles represent kinship groups with which an aboriginal clan, group or individual has a legendary relationship.

Them's the Berriest

With 43,511 tonnes produced in 2002, worth almost $42 million at the farm gate, Canada is the world's largest producer of wild blueberries. Most of the blueberry crop is handpicked.

A Songstress by Any Other Name...

Opera singer Emma Albani (1847–1930), the first Canadian-born international superstar, was born Marie Lajeunesse in Chambly, Québec. During the 1860s, following the rave reviews of her first few public performances in the Montréal, she changed her name to satisfy the public's taste for Italian divas. She went on to worldwide acclaim and settled in England, where she became a Dame of the British Empire. She became Canada's most popular artist of the pre-World War I era.

The King of Corn

Remember Guy Lombardo (1902–77) and the Royal Canadians? Millions of Canadians wouldn't have dreamed of New Year's Eve without them and their bouncy, sing-along version of "Auld Lang Syne." Over Lombardo's long career, the London, ON native sold more than 300 million recordings.

DID YOU  KNOW?

Almost all Canadian grain corn is produced in eastern Canada, with 68% grown in Ontario.

The New Canadian Workhorse

Compared to European workers, Canadians work longer hours, have fewer public holidays, work more overtime, take less time off to raise their children, work more weekends, have fewer vacations and generally retire later. In fact, Canadians work some of the longest hours in the industrialized world.

 Our own Hudson's Bay Company, which received its first Royal Charter in 1670, is the oldest chartered trading company in the world.

ABOUT THE AUTHOR

GWEV Publishing Inc.

ANGELA MURPHY is Angela K. Narth. She is a full-time writer with an extensive and varied background in education. She has held positions as university lecturer, public school administrator, and curriculum consultant before deciding to pursue a career in writing.

Narth has written two non-fiction books, four children's books and several magazine articles. Angela is a free-lance literary reviewer for the *Winnipeg Free Press* and the *Ottawa Citizen*, and her reviews have also been published in *Books in Canada* and *The Gazette* from Montréal. She is a member of the Writers' Union of Canada and the Manitoba Writers' Guild.

BLUE
BIKE
BOOKS

Bathroom Book of Canadian History

From wild weather to strange prime ministers, from the Maritimes to the West Coast, Canada's amazing history is full of the comic, the tragic, and the just plain weird. You'll enjoy this fun collection of fascinating factoids about our peculiar past.

For example:

☞ Fifty-two families in Elgin, MB, had roast goose for dinner the evening of April 22, 1932, after a passing flock was struck by lightning.

☞ Would you believe the Chinese may have discovered Canada centuries before Europeans made the trip?

☞ One of Canada's most famous people never actually existed.

☞ A 17-year-old Torontonian created the most famous superhero of all time.

☞ A herd of Middle Eastern wild camels roamed the western Canadian wilderness for 40 years.

Amaze your friends! Amuse yourself! Pick up your copy of *Bathroom Book of Canadian History* **today!**

Softcover · 5.25" x 8.25" · 144 pages
ISBN-10: 0-9739116-1-1 · ISBN-13: 978-0-9739116-1-9 · **$9.95**

ALSO
COMING SOON!

Weird Canadian Places
&
Bathroom Book of Canadian Quotes